God's Love
For You

Bible Storybook

To:

_____

From:

_____

Date:

_____

BIBLE STORYBOOK

God's Love For You

Rich & Reneé Stearns

Illustrated by Martina Peluso

Bible story adaptations by Carolyn Larsen

Tommy NELSON®

A Division of Thomas Nelson Publishers

NASHVILLE   DALLAS   MEXICO CITY   RIO DE JANEIRO

In Collaboration with World Vision®

World Vision®

Connect your family to God's love around the world

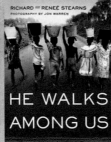

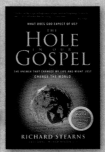

www.worldvision.com

Published in Nashville, Tennessee, by Tommy Nelson. Tommy Nelson is a registered trademark of Thomas Nelson, Inc.

Authors are represented by the literary agency of Alive Communications, Inc., 7680 Goddard Street, Suite 200, Colorado Springs, CO 80920, www.alivecommunications.com.

Illustrated by Martina Peluso.

World Vision Photo Credits
Jon Warren: 19, 62, 63, 76, 77, 85, 88, 89, 100, 101, 104, 116, 117, 140, 141, 144, 156, 157, 164, 165, 168, 169, 178, 179, 190, 191, 202, 224, 228, 243, 246, 265, 271; **Laura Reinhardt:** 22, 38, 39, 108, 148, 149, 160, 242; **Andrea Peer:** 50, 51, 152, 182; **Steve Reynolds:** 34, 35, 92; **Kari Costanza:** 42, 93; **Leonard Makombe:** 96, 97; **Yadira Pacheco:** 70, 71; **Bardha Prendi:** 194, 195; **Makopano Semakale:** 80, 81; **Srinivas:** 66, 67; **World Vision Staff:** 234, 260; **James Addis:** 225; **Amio Ascension:** 128; **Klevisa Breshani:** 264; **Fasil Damte:** 218; **Khalid Hussain:** 29; **Heidi Isaza:** 35; **Hasanthi Jayamaha:** 250; **Collins Kaumba:** 112; **Shirley Kimmayong:** 120; **Sopheak Kong:** 59; **Jon Kubly:** 58; **Cecil Laguardia:** 67; **Alain Mwaku:** 172; **Abby Stalsbroten:** 206; **Jane Sutton-Redner:** 132; **David Ward:** 254

Photo Credits

John M. Curry: 84, 85
Alyssa Bowerman/Cornerstone University: 271
Courtesy of the Bradley Family: 198
Hal Yeager/Genesis Photos: 238

Stock images p#/artist © Shutterstock: 19/catwalker, FloridaStock, 23/MariusdeGraf, Andre Nantel, 29/istockphoto-thinkstock, 35/Rafael Martin-Gaitero, 39/iafoto, 43/Dmitry Saparov, 51/kaband, 59/udeyismail, 71/Wolna, 77/suns07, lawyerphoto, 81/Aleksandar Mijatovic, 85/Guido Amrein, Switzerland, Nathan Holland, 89/mythja, Eric Isselee, Oleg Znamenskiy, 93/PlusONE, 97/hidddenace, 101/ilbusca–istockphoto, 105/arindambanerjee, 109/Attila JANDI, 113/Przemyslaw Skibinski, Georgios Kollidas, 117/africa924, 121/haveseen, 129/Jorg Hackemann, Isa Ismail, 133/Pal Teravagimov, africa924, 145/Ben Heys, Aleksander Mijatovic, 149/Marcel Dufflocq W, 153/Nyord, Dhoxax, 157/Ralf Kleemann, 161/Emi Cristea, Erik Mandre, 165/Eric Isselee, 169/Monika Hrdinova, 173/Photovolcanica.com, 183/Banana Republic Images, 191/Serg64, 195/Dionisvera, 199/Holger Wulschlaeger, AridOcean, 203/FloridaStock, 207/AlenKadr, 219/JM Travel Photography, Dereje, 225/Galyna Andrushko, 229/Dr Morley Read, 235/Boris Stroujko, 239/David Vogt, Eric Gevaert, 243/fckncg, 247/Dereje, Pascal Rateau, 251/joyfull, 255/Racheal Grazias, Dmitry Kalinovsky, 261/mmartin

Cover design by Katie Jennings.

Tommy Nelson titles may be purchased in bulk for educational, business, fund-raising, or sales promotional use. For information, please e-mail SpecialMarkets@ThomasNelson.com.

Library of Congress Cataloging-in-Publication Data

Stearns, Richard (Richard E.)
  God's love for you : Bible storybook / Rich and Reneé Stearns ; illustrated by Martina Peluso.
    pages cm
"In collaboration with World Vision."
ISBN 978-1-4003-2187-2
1. Bible stories, English. I. Peluso, Martina, illustrator. II. Title.
  BS551.3.S725 2013
  220.95'05—dc23   2013007507

Printed in China

13 14 15 16 17 LEO 6 5 4 3 2

To

Sarah, Andy, Hannah, Pete, and Grace
and the thousands of children we've met in our travels
who continue to help us see the
world through God's eyes.

Acknowledgments

We would like to thank the hundreds of World Vision
communicators who work faithfully each day to
capture the important stories of how God is at work
in the lives of His children around the world.

Contents

Old Testament

New Testament

A Letter to Parents

As we sat together playing checkers on his front stoop, we marveled at this boy living alone with his brother and sister in a remote part of Malawi. When George's parents died of AIDS, he became the head of the household. When his termite-infested hut collapsed, he became chief builder. And yet here he was, seemingly without a care in the world, enjoying a game of checkers with his American visitors.

Until we became involved in the work of World Vision, we didn't know any boys like George. We had a pretty limited perspective on the world around us. That's probably true of almost everyone. If the way we spent our time when our kids were growing up is any indication, our world was only as big as the space between our house, the grocery store, our school, our church, and the soccer field. When we have children, our world suddenly becomes very small, with all-consuming, endlessly demanding miniature human beings requiring our attention.

But the truth is, it's a big world out there, full of children who need to know about God's love. While the lyrics "Jesus loves the little children, all the children of the world" acknowledge that children are growing up in places far away from where we live, most of us don't know much about them.

Each year, almost 7 million children under the age of five die because of issues related to their poverty, more than 700 million people go to bed hungry every night, and one person in seven has no access to clean water. As parents, we have a responsibility to prepare our children to love and care for those people in Jesus' name. But how do we do that?

It is our hope that this Bible storybook will be a tool you can use to introduce your child to a bigger world. Our stories and the stories of World Vision's staff members will bring you and your child face-to-face with people who may seem very different from us but are loved by God and, just like us, are those for whom He sent His Son. Their stories are paired with familiar stories from the Bible to demonstrate how God is still at work in the world today, partnering with ordinary people like us to accomplish His purposes.

We often remark that this partnership with God reminds us a little of baking cookies with our kids when they were little. We didn't really need their help measuring and rolling and cutting out all those cookies. We weren't hoping they would provide some expertise in the kitchen that we lacked. In fact, we could have made those cookies much more easily and certainly with a whole lot less mess if we had waited until they were napping.

But that wasn't really the point. There was something so special about working together in the kitchen with our children, something in that activity that was good for all of us. And somehow, mysteriously, we think God feels the same way about partnering with us to do His work in the world. Our prayer is that as you read the stories in this book, you and your child will be encouraged to join in that partnership.

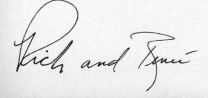

Old Testament

God's Wonderful Creation Plan

Based on **GENESIS 1**

In the beginning, there was no earth, no sky, no land, no plants or animals or people. But God was there. And He had an amazing plan for a world filled with beautiful blue skies and tall green plants and cuddly, funny animals, and—most important—you!

God spoke four powerful words—"Let there be light!"—and creation began. Light burst through the darkness! God called the light *day*, and He called the darkness *night*.

This was the first day, and God was pleased with His work.

On the second day of creation, God separated the land and the sky and made an earth that was ready to receive life. On the third day, He made rugged mountains, green fields, and deep blue oceans. He filled the land with plants—tall trees, juicy fruit and veggie bushes, and big, beautiful flowers. God saw that everything He had made was good.

On the fourth day of creation, God filled the sky with lights. He made the moon and twinkling stars to light the night sky and the bright sun to light the day. God was happy with what He had made.

On the fifth day, God made millions of fish and creatures that live in the water, such as octopuses and sea urchins. He made colorful birds to fly across the sky. God was pleased with this part of His creation too.

The sixth day was very special! God made the animals that live on land. From the tiniest baby bunny to the biggest elephant, from soft lambs to roaring lions, God made them all! And then God made His most important creation . . .

God's wonderful plan was to make a beautiful world for people to enjoy.

He was very happy with everything He had made.

God Made People to Be Like Him

Based on GENESIS 1–2

The final part of God's creation was the most amazing. God said, "Let Us make people in Our own image." He took dust from the ground and shaped it into the first man. Then God blew breath into the man, and he became the first living, breathing human! God named him Adam, and He knew His creation was very good! Then, on the seventh day, God rested.

God had made a beautiful garden for Adam to live in and called it Eden. God said that Adam could eat the yummy fruit from any of the trees in the garden. There was only one tree Adam had to leave alone. God told him not to eat from the tree in the center of the garden—the Tree of Knowledge of Good and Evil. God said, "If you eat fruit from that tree, you will die."

Then God gave Adam a really fun job. Adam got to name all the animals! Whatever Adam called each creature, that became its name. "You shall be a bear. You are a butterfly. I'll call you an elephant. And you? You look like an orangutan!"

God wanted Adam to find a helper and friend for himself, so Adam paid attention as he named the animals. "Nope, not you, Tiger. Nuh-uh, Penguin. You're too hoppy, Kangaroo!" Adam didn't find any animal to be a good friend or helper for him, but God had a plan. He made Adam fall asleep. Then He took one of Adam's ribs and used it to make Eve, the first woman. When Adam saw Eve, he thought she was perfect for him! He said, "She will be my helper and my friend. I will call her *woman*."

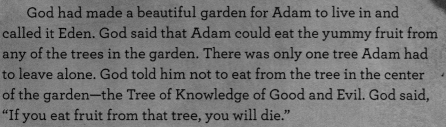

All people are made in God's image.

And God loves every one of us!

God Created Me with Love

As twelve-year-old Teuta pulled open the big wooden church door, she could hardly believe her eyes. Children were laughing and playing, and in one corner boys and girls were reading a book. Teuta wished she could go inside instead of wandering alone around her neighborhood in Tirana, the capital city of Albania.

When Lindita and Marigela looked up and saw the lonely little girl standing at the door, they welcomed her in. Then they introduced her to the other children. It was here that Teuta also met Jesus.

"I felt so good when I read my first book, *God Created Me with Love*," Teuta said. "For the first time, I knew that I was not alone but that I had a Father God in my life, and He hugs me with love and care every time I need Him."

Just like Adam and Eve, every person who has ever lived is a unique creation of God. And God loves us just like He loved Adam and Eve. But sometimes people need a reminder of how special they really are. That's when God calls on people like Lindita and Marigela to tell people like Teuta how much He loves them.

Teuta no longer feels lonely walking around her neighborhood because now she knows where she can go to find friends. She can go to the student center at church, and she can go to her heavenly Father.

"I have learned that God is here anytime I call to Him in prayer."

The center where Teuta learns about God's love.

★ Mother Teresa, who won the Nobel Peace Prize for her work with poor people in India, was from Albania. The national airport is named after her.

★ In addition to the Albanian language, many people speak Greek.

★ Albanians call their country Shqipëria, which means "Land of the Eagles."

Did you KNOW?

Sin is why bad things
like war, hunger, poverty,
and disease exist in this
world. All of us sin, but God
has a plan to
save us from
our sin.

The Beginning of Sin

Based on GENESIS 3

Eve lived with Adam in the garden of Eden. It was so beautiful—perfect even—and it had everything they needed to live. They only had one rule from God: "You can eat from any tree in the garden except one. Do not eat from the Tree of Knowledge of Good and Evil." But as it turned out, even that one rule was too much for Adam and Eve to obey.

One day, a serpent asked Eve, "Did God say that you can't eat fruit from *any* of the trees in the garden?"

"Of course we can eat fruit," Eve answered. "We can eat all the fruit we want, except from that tree in the middle of the garden. God said not to eat its fruit. In fact, we can't even touch it or we will die."

"You won't die. God wasn't serious about that," the serpent said. "God knows that if you eat that fruit, you will learn about good and evil. You will be wise like He is."

Hmm, Eve thought. *That fruit does look yummy.* She grabbed a piece and took a big, juicy bite. "Adam! Try this! It's so good!" she cried out. Adam took a bite too. Right away they both knew they had broken God's one rule. And they were ashamed.

Later, as He was walking through the garden, God called out to Adam, "Where are you?" But Adam and Eve were hiding. God already knew they had disobeyed Him. They had sinned.

God told Adam and Eve they would have to leave the perfect garden of Eden.

God was very sad that sin and death had entered the world He had created, but He had a plan that would show people, His most special creation, how much He loved them.

The Good News That Jesus Forgives Sin!

Have you ever had to move to a new neighborhood or a new school? It can be hard to find friends. Now imagine how hard it would be to move to a new country where you don't even speak the language.

That's how it was for Juan when he moved from El Salvador to the United States. Juan spoke Spanish, but everyone else spoke English. That made him feel really lonely, so he started looking for new friends. He met a group of kids who did bad things like fighting and stealing, and they convinced Juan to join them.

But then Juan got an afterschool job working in a restaurant for a nice lady. "Juan," she said one day while he was working, "did you know that whatever bad things you've done in the past can be forgiven?"

This was good news, and Juan wanted to know more. He had done a lot of bad things. "God loves you so much," she explained, "that He sent His Son, Jesus, to save you and me and anyone else who will receive His love."

Juan liked that idea very much, so he prayed that Jesus would forgive his sins and make Juan part of His family. And of course Jesus said, "Yes!"

Juan (left) now helps other people love and serve God.

Did you KNOW?

★ In 1969, El Salvador went to war with neighboring Honduras over the outcome of a soccer game. The war lasted 100 hours.

★ El Salvador has 22 volcanoes, many of them still active. The country is known as the "Land of the Volcanoes."

Noah obeyed God even though His instructions were unusual.

And God kept His promise to protect Noah and his family.

Noah's Big Boat

Based on GENESIS 6–7

Noah!" God called. "There's a flood coming—a big, big flood. It's going to wipe out everything—towns, people, plants, *everything*! I want you to be safe, so build a very big boat. I'll tell you exactly how to make it."

God was angry about the way people were behaving. They were selfish, they were mean to one another, and they didn't care at all about serving Him. God had tried to get the people to listen to Him and change how they lived, but no one paid any attention except Noah. He had always tried to obey God. That's why God wanted Noah to be safe from the big flood.

"And you can bring your family, Noah," God told him. "But I also want you to bring animals."

Animals? Wild animals? How many animals? Noah wondered.

"I want you to bring lots of animals. I'm sending two of every kind of animal on the earth to go into the boat. Take enough food for them and for your family," God said.

Even though there wasn't a rain cloud in the sky, Noah got busy sawing and hammering to make the big boat exactly the way God had told him to.

Not long after he finished building the boat, Noah heard the *clomp, clomp, clomp* of a big parade of animals marching toward the boat. Noah stepped aside as every kind of animal in the world flew and hopped and stomped into the big boat. Then he and his family followed them inside.

God shut the door of the big boat just as it began to rain—and it rained and rained and rained. When he saw the waters begin to rise, Noah took a deep breath and whispered a prayer of thanks for God's amazing protection.

God Keeps His Promises

Based on GENESIS 8–9

*P*link! Plink! Plink! Raindrops pounded against the big wooden boat. Waves rocked it back and forth, back and forth. *How long are we going to be in here?* Noah wondered. *It's getting really stinky, and I sure am tired of cleaning up after the animals.*

Noah and his family had been in the boat for forty days, and it had rained the entire time! Outside, the water had risen higher and higher, until everything was under water. Everything on land had been destroyed, but Noah and his family and the animals on the big boat were safe.

Then one day, no more raindrops could be heard pounding against the boat. The rain had finally stopped!

Each day, the floodwaters got a little bit lower, and finally the boat came to rest on top of a mountain. But now the earth was a giant mud pit. Noah and his family had to wait until the land dried before it was safe for them to leave the boat.

When Noah finally opened the boat's big door, the bunnies, deer, elephants, and tigers came racing out. They were happy to be free, and the warm sunshine felt so good!

Noah built an altar and gathered his family around it to thank God for His protection.

"Noah," God said, "I promise I will never again send a flood big enough to cover the whole world. This rainbow I'm putting in the sky is a sign of My promise."

When God makes a promise, He always keeps it.

Lots of Rain—and Lots of Help

Mozambique is a big country in southeast Africa. Most people who live there are farmers. Rain is good for farms, but one time it rained so hard that all the farmland was underwater! Rosa and her four children watched as the water rose from their knees to their waists and then all the way up to their necks! What were they going to do?

Rosa told her children to climb into a tall tree, and she tied ropes around their waists so they wouldn't fall out. Unfortunately, because of the flood, snakes also crawled up into the tree, and Rosa and the children had to beat them away with branches! Then they watched as everything they owned—their crops, goats, chickens, cows, and even their house—was washed away by the terrible flood.

After Rosa and her family spent four long days in the tree, a helicopter rescued them. But now they needed a new house, new animals, and new seeds to plant. The children also needed clothes and books. That's when some Christian friends came to help. They gave Rosa seeds and a loan so she could replace the things the family had lost.

God promised Noah that He would never again send a flood to destroy the whole earth, and He kept that promise. Rosa's family was able to start over.

God sent kind Christian workers to remind Rosa and her children that God loves them and that He can be trusted.

In many countries, floods force families out of their homes. These people in Pakistan are waiting for help.

Did you KNOW?

★ Elephants, buffalo, zebras, hippopotamuses, lions, crocodiles, and over 300 species of birds live in Mozambique.

★ Children in Mozambique like to eat rice topped with spicy stew, fresh fruit, and posho (a porridge made out of corn) for lunch.

Abram Follows God

Based on **GENESIS 12; 15**

A bram," God called. "Pack up your stuff, and get ready to go."
I will obey God, Abram thought, *but I wonder where He wants me to go?*

God continued, "I promise to make you into a great nation. I will bless you, and I will bless all the families on earth through you."

So Abram and his wife, Sarai, packed all their belongings. They took their servants and their animals and started on a journey, trusting God to guide them. Abram's nephew Lot went along with his servants and his animals.

God led them to Canaan, where He told Abram, "I promise to give this land to your children and to their children after that." *That's a wonderful promise*, Abram may have thought, *but Sarai and I don't have any children.*

God said, "Abram, look around at this land. I am giving it to you. As far as you can see to the north, south, east, and west—all this land will be yours. And yes, you will have a big family. You will have as many descendants as there are stars in the sky!"

Abram trusted God so much that he followed where God led.

God Is True to His Word

Based on **GENESIS 17–18, 21**

Abram and Sarai had faithfully obeyed God. They had left behind everything they'd ever known and followed Him. God had promised them a big family, and they had believed Him. But now they were both very old, and they still did not have even one child. It was difficult for them to be patient.

That's when God went to Abram again and said, "Your name will now be *Abraham*. It means 'father of many nations.' Sarai will now be *Sarah*, and she will give you a son."

But still they waited.

And waited.

Abraham and Sarah must have wondered if they had misunderstood God's promise. But they were about to be amazed!

Three men appeared with a special message from God: "By this time next year, Abraham, your wife will have a baby boy."

Abraham didn't know what to say. But Sarah laughed to herself as she thought, *Now? I've waited my entire life to be a mother! And now that I'm old—now I will have a baby?*

Sure enough, a few months later Sarah became pregnant. The miracle of a baby growing inside her made her smile. God had kept His promise in a miraculous way, and Sarah gave birth to a baby boy! Abraham and Sarah finally had the child God had promised them. They named their little boy Isaac, which means "laughter."

Just as God said, Abraham's descendants *are* like the stars in the sky—there are too many to count! Many years after Isaac was born, the most important Son would be born through Abraham's family. But first, Abraham had Isaac, and Isaac had Jacob and Esau, and Jacob had . . . well, Jacob had *twelve* sons!

Never give up on God—even when you have to wait a really long time! God will not forget you. He will not leave you, and He will always do exactly what He says.

God Is Faithful!

Francisco loved living in the mountains. Goats and sheep and llamas wandered everywhere. The rocks and cliffs were his playground. Life in the Andes Mountains of Peru was almost perfect.

But then Francisco's father died, and his mother, Octaviana, was left all by herself to tend their fields, care for the livestock, and raise Francisco and his brother and sister.

Octaviana couldn't do it alone. Even in good times, running the home was hard work. But now she had no help. Francisco and his brother and sister did what they could, but they were little. Then the animals got sick, and the crops dried up. Octaviana didn't know what to do.

But she remembered that God loves His children and promised never to leave them alone. So she began to pray, "God, do not forget me and my children on this mountain. Please send help."

Then Octaviana waited. The seasons changed, more animals got sick, and it became more and more difficult to grow enough food to feed the family. Still, Octaviana waited and prayed.

Then one morning Octaviana saw some workers from World Vision walking up the trail that ran beside her house. They had come to help! They wanted to do something to make Octaviana's life better. They helped her care for the sick animals and plant healthy crops. They made sure that Francisco, his brother, and his sister had enough food to eat and could return to school. Octaviana had patiently waited for God's help, and He had answered her prayers!

God used Rich and Reneé Stearns to help answer Octaviana's prayers.

Did you KNOW?

★ The largest lake by volume in South America is Lake Titicaca. It is located on the border between Peru and Bolivia.

★ The Andes is the second highest mountain range in the world. At 22,205 feet tall, Mount Huascarán is the highest peak in Peru.

★ People in Peru use tall, furry animals called llamas to carry heavy things from place to place.

Joseph the Dreamer

Based on **GENESIS 37; 41**

Jacob had twelve sons, but one son—Joseph—was his favorite. Jacob treated Joseph differently than he treated his other sons. One time, Jacob gave Joseph a special colorful coat to wear. It was nicer than anything Joseph's brothers had, and this made them angry.

One night, Joseph had a dream, and he told his brothers about it. "I dreamed we were working in the field when suddenly my bundle of grain rose up taller than your bundles. Then all your bundles of grain bowed down to mine." Joseph had a second dream where the sun and the moon and eleven stars (like Joseph's eleven brothers) bowed down to him.

"Do you think we are going to bow down to you? Do you think you are ever going to rule over us?" the brothers shouted angrily.

One day, as the brothers were watching their father's sheep, they came up with a plan to murder Joseph. But Reuben said, "We don't have to kill Joseph. Let's toss him in that deep hole over there."

Not long after they dropped Joseph into the hole, the brothers saw a caravan of people heading toward Egypt. "Here's an idea," one of them suggested. "Let's sell Joseph to them. He can be a slave, and we'll be rid of him."

Poor Joseph! One day he was enjoying being his father's favorite son, and the next day he was being thrown into a deep hole and then sent off to Egypt. But God was always with him, and God took care of Joseph wherever he went.

While in Egypt, Joseph lived in a way that pleased God. So God blessed Joseph, and he went from being a slave to being the governor of Egypt!

Joseph trusted God because he knew that, whether things are good or bad, God is still with us.

God Sends Help

One minute they had a perfectly good house, and the next minute it was gone!

A storm with terrible winds and a dark funnel-shaped cloud hit the town of Holt, Alabama, and destroyed the house where Christian, Jimena, and Maria Guadalupe lived with their parents. The tornado blew so hard that everything they owned was carried away—their furniture, their clothing, even their toys!

Five-year-old Christian didn't understand what had happened. "Where are we going to live now? Where are our toys?" he cried.

His mother hugged him and told Christian that even though they had lost a lot, they had friends who were going to help their family start over. Soon they were able to get a new house. Christian's new room was painted blue. The room that Jimena and Maria Guadalupe shared was pink.

The town had a big carnival so the children who had lost everything could get ready to go back to school. Each child received a backpack filled with school supplies, new shoes, and a toy. Volunteers also included handwritten notes so that Christian, his sisters, and all their friends would know that people they had never even met cared about them and were praying for them!

God is always with us, even when life is hard. April 27, 2011, was a terrible day for the people of Holt. But God brought kind and generous people into their lives to help them begin again.

After a terrible storm, Christian (center) has a new home, and children have school supplies.

★ Tornadoes are sometimes called twisters.

★ The city of Tuscaloosa, Alabama, got its name from two Choctaw Indian words meaning "black warrior."

★ The University of Alabama football team is called the Crimson Tide. This nickname comes from a famous football game played in red mud.

God Turns Joseph's Troubles to Good

Based on GENESIS 41–45

I've got to find food for my family. We'll soon starve to death, Jacob thought. The land of Canaan hadn't had any rain for so long that all the crops had died. When the animals couldn't find food, they died too. Soon, people in Canaan would die from hunger as well.

But the neighboring country of Egypt had huge storehouses overflowing with food. Egypt had all this food because Joseph had listened to the message God had sent to Pharaoh in a dream, and Joseph had been busy storing up plenty of grain. Starving people from other countries were going to Egypt to buy, trade, or beg for food.

That's why, back in Canaan, Joseph's father, Jacob, told his other sons, "Go to Egypt. Buy grain and bring it here. Leave now before we all starve to death."

In Egypt, the brothers waited in line to buy food from the man in charge. They didn't know that the man was their long-lost brother—the one *they* had sold into slavery. Joseph recognized them, but they didn't recognize him!

Not until after they had gone home to Canaan with a load of grain and then returned to Egypt for more food did Joseph let them in on his secret. "Brothers, don't you know me? It's me, Joseph."

Uh-oh, the brothers thought. *We're in big trouble now!* They were afraid to even look at their brother.

But Joseph said, "Don't be afraid. It's true that you did bad things to me. But God turned your bad actions into good, and now I can save your life! Go get Dad. You can live here in Egypt, and I will take care of you!"

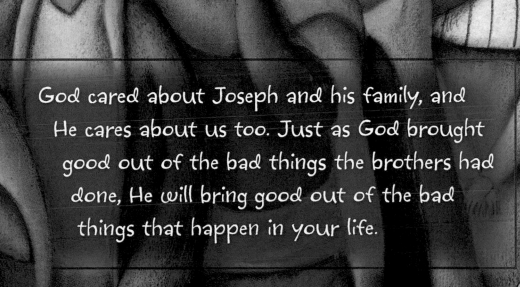

God cared about Joseph and his family, and He cares about us too. Just as God brought good out of the bad things the brothers had done, He will bring good out of the bad things that happen in your life.

NIGER

Hope in the Middle of a Famine

Niger is one of the poorest countries in the world, partly because of its location on the edge of a big desert. It almost never rains, so farmers have a hard time growing crops. That means there isn't always enough food for everyone to eat. When that happens, it's called a *famine*, like the one that took place in Egypt during Joseph's lifetime.

People need food to stay healthy, but during a famine, many people get sick, especially children. That's what happened to Sahabi Ibrahim. From the time he was born, Sahabi Ibrahim didn't have enough food to eat, so he was very, very small. His mother was worried about her son and took him to a hospital in the town of Maradi, where a nurse could take care of him.

Sahabi Ibrahim's mother was very hopeful that he would get better, and the nurse was too. She explained that the little boy just needed more food so he could grow big and strong. Like Joseph, the people at the hospital had made plans so they would have enough food to help children like Sahabi Ibrahim.

Sahabi Ibrahim's mother wants him to go to school, learn English, and eventually become a nurse so he can return to his village and help others who become sick when a famine strikes. She would like Sahabi Ibrahim to care for others the same way Joseph cared for his family.

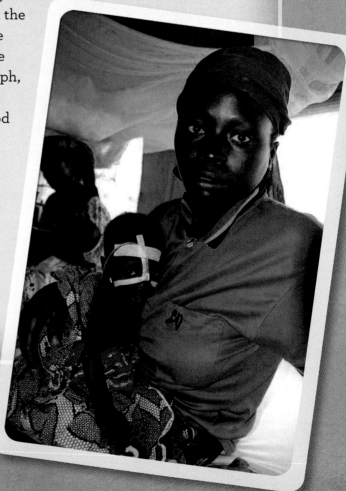

Without enough rain to grow food, little Sahabi Ibrahim became very hungry and sick.

★ Over 80% of Niger is located in the Sahara Desert, the third largest desert in the world.

★ Niger is one of the hottest places on earth, so it has the nickname "Frying Pan of the World."

Did you KNOW?

God always has a plan. Sometimes it's hard to see, and that's when it is important to trust Him.

Moses Is Born

Based on EXODUS 1–2

Joseph's family got bigger and bigger, and all of his children and grandchildren and great-grandchildren were called the Hebrew people. Hundreds of years later, so many Hebrews were living in Egypt that the new pharaoh was afraid they would try to take over his country. So he ordered all the Hebrew baby boys in Egypt to be killed.

For three months, one Hebrew mother kept her baby boy hidden. But as the baby got older, it got harder for her to hide him. He could be very noisy!

I cannot just let my son die, the woman thought to herself. *I have to do something to protect him . . . I know what I'll do. I'll weave a basket and cover it with tar to make a little boat.* Then the woman gently laid her little boy in the basket and carried it down to the Nile River. She set the basket on the water, and the baby's sister, Miriam, stayed by the river to see what would happen.

Soon the Egyptian princess came to the river with her servants. The princess saw the basket floating on the water and sent a servant to get it. She opened it and said, "Look! It's a Hebrew baby."

Miriam ran to the princess. "Would you like me to get a Hebrew woman to take care of the baby for you?" she asked.

The princess said yes. Miriam couldn't believe the princess was saving her little brother's life. She raced home. "Momma! Come with me. The princess found our baby. She wants you to care for him!"

The princess kept him as her son and named the baby Moses, which means "I drew him out of the water."

Moses the Leader

Based on EXODUS 2–12

When he was a young man, Moses ran away from Egypt. Moses had killed an Egyptian who was hurting a Hebrew slave, and Moses was afraid of what Pharaoh might do to him.

One day Moses was out in a field watching sheep when he noticed a bush on fire. But even though it burned and burned, it did not burn up.

When Moses moved closer to investigate this strange sight, he heard a voice coming from inside the bush: "Moses! Moses!" God was calling to him from the burning bush! "Don't come any closer. Take off your shoes. You are standing on holy ground." Then God gave Moses an important job: "I want you to lead My people out of slavery in Egypt."

Moses hid his face. *Oh, not me! I don't know how to do that job!* Moses thought. Out loud he said, "Why would Pharaoh listen to me?"

God spoke to Moses. "What's that in your hand?"

"My shepherd's staff," Moses answered. God told him to throw it down on the ground. When Moses did, it became a snake. God told him to pick it up, and when he did, it became a staff again.

"I'll help you do miracles so the people will know I am with you," God said. But Moses was still nervous because he couldn't speak well, so God agreed to let his brother, Aaron, go along to be his helper.

Moses and Aaron went to the pharaoh of Egypt and announced, "God says to let His people go."

But Pharaoh said no, so God made all the water in Egypt turn to blood.

Moses went back to Pharaoh and again asked him to let the people go. Pharaoh said no again. Ten times Moses asked, ten times Pharaoh said no, and ten times God sent a plague to show His great power. The last plague was so bad that Pharaoh told Moses to take the Hebrew people out of Egypt!

God told Moses to look at what was in his hand. Moses had what he needed to do the work God had given him to do. God will always give His people the tools we need to do the work He gives us.

What's in Your Hand?

The only thing Moses had when God told him to lead the Israelites out of Egypt was a staff, an ordinary stick he used to lead sheep around in the desert.

The only thing Austin Gutwein had was a basketball. Austin was really good at shooting baskets, and that gave him an idea.

When Austin heard about some children in Africa whose parents had died, he wanted to do something to help them. But what could a nine-year-old boy do to make a difference in the lives of kids who lived thousands of miles from his home in Mesa, Arizona? *Well*, Austin thought, *I could earn money for those children by shooting free throws!*

And that's what he did. Austin began an organization called Hoops of Hope, and he got children all over the world to join him. All these kids found sponsors who would donate money for every free throw they made, and they raised enough money to build a school in Kalomo, Zambia.

But the Hoops of Hope kids didn't stop there. In ten years, Hoops of Hope and more than 40,000 children raised enough money to build two medical clinics in Zambia and four dormitories. All of this happened because, like Moses, a young boy used what he had in his hand. It was only a basketball, but with it, Austin has helped to change the world.

Austin has made a big difference in Zambia just by shooting basketballs.

Did you KNOW?

★ Zambians eat *nshima* (ground cornmeal) at least once a day. They form it into a ball and dip it into cooked vegetables or soup.

★ The world's largest edible mushroom— and it can be up to three feet wide!—grows in Zambia.

No matter how bad things seem to be sometimes, trust God

He can do amazing miracles to protect His people.

52

God Parts the Sea

Based on EXODUS 14

After Pharaoh ordered the Hebrews to leave, the Egyptians didn't have any slaves. "What have we done by letting the Hebrews go? Who will make our bricks for us? Who will take care of our houses and do all the work?"

Pharaoh decided he wanted the Hebrews back in Egypt. So he climbed into his chariot and ordered all the chariots of his army to go after the Hebrew people.

God had been leading His people with a pillar of cloud during the day and a pillar of fire at night. But when the Hebrews saw the dust kicked up by the Egyptian army following them, they were terrified. "Oh no! Moses, you should have left us in slavery! Do something to save us!" the people shouted.

As the Egyptian army got closer and closer, the Hebrews became more and more frightened! Moses said, "Don't be afraid. Just wait and see what God will do to save you!"

God told Moses to hold his shepherd's staff over the Red Sea. When he did, a powerful wind began to blow, and it blew the water into two big walls! Then the Hebrews marched through the Red Sea on dry ground as the giant walls of water stood tall on either side of them!

Moses held out his staff while thousands of Hebrews crossed the Red Sea! As the last Hebrew came out of the sea on one side, the Egyptian army raced in on the other side, confident that they could catch their former slaves. But Moses lowered his shepherd's staff, and the water came crashing down on the Egyptian soldiers. The Egyptian army was wiped out—and God's people were all safe on the other side of the Red Sea.

Trials and Tablets in the Desert

Based on EXODUS 16–17; 20

God had done amazing things for the Hebrews. He had done miracles to free them from the Egyptians. He had opened the sea so they could walk through it. But still they forgot to thank God, and still they didn't fully trust Him. One time the people whined that they were hungry. "You should have left us in Egypt, Moses! At least we had food to eat there!"

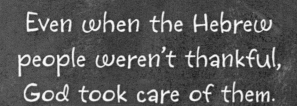

Even when the Hebrew people weren't thankful, God took care of them.

Moses asked God for help, and God sent food from heaven. This food—called *manna*—appeared on the ground every morning, and the people ate it every day for years and years. But they weren't very thankful.

Another time the people complained that they were thirsty. God told Moses to hit a certain rock with his shepherd staff. When Moses did, water poured right out from the rock! The people had water to drink! God had taken care of them again.

One day, the Hebrew people camped near Mount Sinai. God called Moses to come up to the top of the mountain. He wanted to give Moses some important rules to live by so that the Hebrew people would know how to please God.

- Love God more than you love anything or anyone else.
- Do not make idols to worship.
- Use God's name with love and respect.
- Remember the Lord's Day, and keep it holy.
- Honor your father and mother.
- Do not murder.
- Be faithful to your husband or wife.
- Do not steal.
- Do not lie.
- Do not want the stuff your neighbor has.

Sometimes it may seem that God is asking you to do something crazy. But if He asks you to do it, take Him seriously and obey, even if others tease or make fun.

Joshua and the Battle of Jericho

Based on JOSHUA 6

After Moses died, Joshua became the leader of the Hebrew people. By then God had taken them to the land He had promised Abraham long ago. Now the people needed to capture Jericho, a powerful city with a big, thick wall around it. How would the Hebrews get into the city, much less conquer it?

They couldn't go over the wall.

They couldn't go through the wall.

They certainly couldn't go under the wall.

But God had a plan!

"Joshua," God said, "this is how I want you to capture Jericho. Take the people, and march around the city once a day for six days. Have seven priests carry horns. On the seventh day, march around the city seven times. When the horns blast, have the people shout, and the wall will collapse."

Walk around the city? Shout? How could *that* make the wall fall down? The people of Jericho would stand on the wall and make fun of them!

Even though God's instructions seemed crazy, Joshua told the people to follow them anyway. And that's just what they did. Once a day for six days, Joshua led the people around the walls of Jericho. There was no sound except the *stomp, stomp, stomp* of their feet and the loud blare of the priests' horns. The people of Jericho must have wondered what on earth the Hebrews were doing. They would soon find out!

On the seventh day, the Hebrews marched around the city just as they had the previous six days. But this time they didn't stop. They went around Jericho again and again—seven times. Then the priests gave one final long blast on their horns, the Hebrews shouted, and the big wall around Jericho crumbled to the ground! The Hebrews rushed in and captured the city!

Crazy Obedience

"The president of World Vision has bought a giant ship!" people said. "What on earth is he going to do with that?"

Stan Mooneyham believed that God wanted him to rescue families who had escaped from a terrible war in Southeast Asia. They had run from the fighting in their country and were floating in small, rickety boats on the South China Sea. The only way Mr. Mooneyham could think to help was to get a ship, sail to the South China Sea, and find them. People thought he was crazy! What did he know about ships?

One of the people Mr. Mooneyham rescued was Vinh Chung, a four-year-old boy who fled Vietnam with his parents and seven brothers and sisters. Imagine what it must have been like bobbing around in the middle of the ocean in that crowded little boat—and how happy they must have been to see Mr. Mooneyham's ship sailing toward them. Vinh's family was safe at last!

Rescued from the water by Mr. Mooneyham, Vinh's family moved to the United States, where people from a church helped them find a home and told them about Jesus. One by one, every member of the family fell in love with Jesus and tried hard to obey Him, just as Mr. Mooneyham had obeyed God when he bought that ship.

Now Vinh is grown up, and he works as a doctor, helping sick people get better. He and his wife and children are thankful that Mr. Mooneyham bought that big ship, even though at the time it seemed like a pretty crazy thing to do.

This is the boat that rescued Vinh—now he's a doctor who helps children (facing page).

Did you KNOW?

★ There are more than 33 million motorbikes in Vietnam!

★ Gongs, not bells, are used to call children to class in Vietnamese schools.

★ Vietnamese people use fishing poles to fish for lizards—and it's more popular than fishing for fish!

Ruth and Naomi

Based on THE BOOK OF RUTH

It's time for me to go back home to Bethlehem, Naomi decided. Many years had gone by since her family had moved to Moab in search of food. A terrible famine had struck their homeland in Israel, but now the famine was over. Still, Naomi was very sad. While they were living in Moab, her husband and both her sons had died, and she was returning to Bethlehem without them.

"Oh, I will miss you!" Naomi told her daughters-in-law, Orpah and Ruth. "Go back to your own families—and may God show kindness to you. Maybe you will marry again."

Orpah hugged and kissed Naomi and returned to her family. But Ruth refused to leave Naomi. "I'll go wherever you go," Ruth promised. "Your people will be my people. Your God will be the God I serve." But Naomi knew that she could not take care of Ruth or do anything to help her. After all, Naomi had no other sons for Ruth to marry. But Ruth was determined. She was not going to leave her mother-in-law!

So Ruth and Naomi traveled to Bethlehem. When they got there, Ruth went to work in a field picking up leftover grain so she and Naomi would have some food. Ruth worked very hard, and Boaz, the owner of the field, noticed. He was impressed with how hard Ruth worked to take care of Naomi. "May God bless you and reward you for what you have done," he said to Ruth.

Boaz wanted to help Ruth. He made sure there was plenty of grain lying in the field for Ruth to pick up so that she and Naomi could eat. Then later, Boaz married Ruth!

Just as Ruth had taken care of Naomi, God took care of Ruth. Soon after she married Boaz, they had a little boy named Obed. What a blessing he was to his dad and mom—and what a blessing Obed was to Grandma Naomi!

Being part of a family is a blessing from God. Family members encourage, love, and help one another.

God may not speak to you out loud like He spoke to Samuel. But He speaks to us through the Bible, through His people (like Mom and Dad and Sunday school teachers), and in our hearts. If we follow what God tells us, we can be great servants for Him.

Young Samuel Hears God

Based on 1 SAMUEL 1; 3

"S amuel!"

Samuel sat up in bed. Who was calling him?

Samuel was a young boy who lived at the temple, where Eli, the priest, was teaching him to serve God. Before he was born, Samuel's mother had prayed and had promised God that if He would give her a baby, she would give him back to God for His service. God answered her prayer, and Hannah kept her promise. When Samuel was old enough, Hannah took him to live at the temple.

After Samuel heard his name called, he jumped out of bed and ran to Eli. "Here I am, sir. What do you need?" he asked.

"I didn't call you," Eli said. "Go back to bed."

Samuel went back to bed and was nearly asleep when he heard the voice again. "Samuel!"

Again Samuel jumped up and ran to Eli. "Here I am. Did you call me?" he asked.

"No, I didn't call you," Eli said. "Go back to bed." So Samuel went back to bed.

Once again he was nearly asleep when he heard, "Samuel! Samuel!"

The boy ran into Eli's room again and said, "Here I am. Did you call me?"

Now Eli realized what was happening. He said, "Samuel, it is God who is calling you. Go back to bed, and if you hear your name called again, say, 'Here I am, Lord. I am listening to You.'"

Samuel went back to bed and waited. Sure enough, the Lord called him again: "Samuel! Samuel!"

"I'm here, Lord," Samuel answered. "I am listening."

Samuel listened to God and then obeyed what God told him to do. When Samuel grew up, he continued to listen to God and became a great prophet who told people about God and His plan for their lives.

INDIA

A Young Girl Brings Words of Hope

Where is Chamabenna? Manjula wondered. He had not been in school for days. Manjula hoped he was not ill. She was afraid it could be something even worse.

In Holtikoti, India, where Manjula lives, poor parents often depend on their children to help earn money for the family, so children leave school to get a job. That is exactly what had happened to Manjula's friend Chamabenna. He had gone to work on a local plantation to help the farmer grow his crops. When Manjula found out, she was very sad, so she decided to go to Chamabenna's home and talk to his parents.

Just as God used Samuel to deliver important messages to the people of Israel, God used Manjula to tell her friend's parents about how much God loves children and about how important it is to allow them to stay in school. It took courage for her to talk with Chamabenna's mom and dad, but they were willing to hear what she had to say. Then she invited them to the World Vision Children's Club. There they learned how they could receive help so they could send their son back to school.

Manjula's community is happy that she is helping other children. Her words give parents hope and encouragement that they can provide for their families without sending their children to work on the plantations.

"We were glad [Chamabenna's] parents were open-minded and listened to us even though we were children," Manjula said. "It was a good feeling to have been listened to."

Did you KNOW?

★ India is home to over 1.2 billion people. That's more people than any other country except China.

★ To nod "yes" in India, you tilt your head left to right—almost like shaking your head "no" in the US!

Manjula stood up for her friend Chamabenna so he could stay in school.

David's Servant Heart

Based on 1 SAMUEL 16

God ordered Samuel to go to Bethlehem and visit a man named Jesse because He had chosen one of Jesse's sons to be the next king of Israel. "How can I go?" Samuel asked. "If King Saul hears about my finding a new king, he will have me killed!"

Still, Samuel obeyed God and headed out for Bethlehem to meet Jesse and his sons. When Samuel saw Jesse's son Eliab, he thought, *This must be the son God has chosen to be king.* But God said, "No, he's not the one. I don't look at how handsome or strong or tall a man is. I look at his heart."

Then came Abinadab, another of Jesse's sons. God said, "No, I have not chosen this one either." Samuel met seven of Jesse's sons, but none of them was the one God had chosen to be king.

"Do you have any other sons?" Samuel asked Jesse.

"Yes, the youngest is out in the field watching the sheep," Jesse said.

"Send for him," Samuel instructed.

When David came in, God said to Samuel, "This is the one. This boy will one day be king."

God chose David because He saw that, in his heart, David wanted to serve Him. So Samuel anointed David to become the king after Saul's reign ended. From that day forward, God's Spirit was with David.

God doesn't care how strong or important a person is. God chooses people whose hearts long to serve and obey Him.

Looking at the Heart

Luz Marina's house didn't have a stove, so her mother cooked the family's meals inside over a small open fire. She had never had any problem before, but one day something happened, and the fire became a huge blaze. Flames raced through Luz Marina's home, leaving her badly burned. But when a group of visitors came to visit Quiquijana, Luz Marina's village high in the Andes Mountains of Peru, the community chose the seven-year-old little girl with the scars to be part of the group that welcomed them.

The fire had burned Luz Marina's face, she now walked with a limp, and it was hard for her to raise her arm above her head. When she opened her mouth to sing, though, Luz Marina seemed like a different person. No one noticed her burns anymore. Everyone was focused on her beautiful voice. No wonder she had been chosen to represent her village as part of the welcoming committee! Her song made everyone feel happy. Regardless of the harm the fire had done to Luz Marina on the outside, her heart was full of love and joy on the inside—and it showed!

When God asked Samuel to find the next king He had chosen to lead Israel, Samuel thought God would pick Jesse's strongest and most handsome son. But God explained to Samuel that He doesn't care what people look like on the outside. As is true about Luz Marina, what is most important about us is what's in our hearts.

God sees the beauty of Luz Marina, despite her burns.

Did you KNOW?

★ The *potato* is originally from Peru. There are almost 4,000 native varieties of Peruvian potatoes.

★ Peru is home to over 1,800 species of *birds*, one of the most in any country in the world.

Little David Fights Big Goliath

Based on 1 SAMUEL 17

"Send your best soldier to fight me!" the Philistine giant named Goliath yelled. "If he wins, we'll be your servants. If I win, you serve us!"

Every day for forty days, Goliath shouted at King Saul's army. And at nine feet tall, dressed in armor, and holding a huge spear, Goliath was scary! The Israelite soldiers were terribly afraid. Even when Goliath made fun of God, none of King Saul's soldiers would fight him.

David's father sent him to take supplies to his brothers, who were soldiers in King Saul's army. David heard Goliath shouting and was surprised that no one stepped forward to fight the giant. So David marched up to King Saul and volunteered: "I'll fight him."

"You can't fight him," King Saul said. "You're just a boy."

"I've killed lions and bears to protect my sheep," David responded. "This giant is challenging the army of God. I will beat him too!"

"Okay," King Saul reluctantly agreed, "but at least wear my armor."

David put on the armor, but it was too big. David could barely move! So he took it off, picked up five smooth stones, and grabbed his slingshot.

When the giant saw a young boy coming to fight him, he got angry. "Come on! I'll feed you to the birds!" Goliath roared.

David wasn't afraid. He knew he wasn't alone. David knew God was on his side. "You have a sword and a spear, but I am fighting in the name of the Lord God Almighty!" David called. He put a stone in his sling and flung it at Goliath. The stone hit the giant in the forehead, and he fell to the ground. David won with only a slingshot . . . and the power of God!

David knew what all the adult soldiers in King Saul's army had forgotten. He wasn't fighting alone; God was with him. And God is stronger than any problem, even a giant problem!

Based on 1 SAMUEL 25

Nabal was a very grouchy man. In fact, he was downright mean! He owned a big farm and had thousands of animals. He even had a beautiful and smart wife named Abigail. But still he was foolish and grumpy.

David had not yet become king of Israel when he and his men were near Nabal's land. David sent messengers to Nabal. "Sir, we are with your servant David. We were camped near your shepherds. We protected them and were good to them. Anything you could spare for us now would be very much appreciated."

But Nabal said, "Who is David? Why should I give you food? I won't give you anything!"

Abigail was a peacemaker who kept David from doing something he would be sorry for later.

74

When the men reported what Nabal had said, David got angry. "Strap on your swords! We're going after him!" David and four hundred men headed for Nabal's farm.

A servant told Abigail what Nabal had done. "Quick!" she said. "Gather food and drink! Load it on a donkey. I'm going to see David."

As Abigail bowed before David, she said, "Sir, I take the blame for how my husband treated your servants. I didn't know your men had come to ask for food, but God has kept you from violence. Don't let my husband's foolishness cause you to sin. Please accept these gifts from me."

"Praise God! And may you be blessed for your wisdom! You have kept me from hurting people today," David said, and he sent Abigail home in peace. When she told Nabal what happened, his heart turned to stone and he died.

When David heard this news, he sent a message to Abigail asking her to be his wife, and she happily said yes.

A peacemaker helps people get along better.

COLOMBIA

Children Working for Peace

Mayerly Sanchez could never play outside. Her hometown of Bogotá, Colombia, was not a safe place to live. People were always fighting. Not even the children were safe!

The way people treated one another made Mayerly very sad. She wanted the fighting to stop, but the adults were not doing enough to make things better. So even though she was a child, Mayerly organized peace parades, talked to government officials, and began a club where children could learn what it means to be peaceful. She helped them to understand that living peacefully begins at home. This national children's peace movement was nominated for a Nobel Prize, the most important award for peace in the world.

Adults began to pay attention to the children. They listened when the children spoke, and when the children marched in the streets, people cheered. Colombia still isn't a very safe place to live, but it is getting better because of the work of Mayerly and her friends in the Children's Movement for Peace in Colombia. Mayerly and her friends did not win the Nobel Peace Prize, but they are still making progress!

"We define *peace* in four words: *love, acceptance, forgiveness*, and *work*," Mayerly explained. And even though she was young, she helped make her country more peaceful. Mayerly is a good example of a peacemaker for other children and for adults as well!

Mayerly bravely spoke up for peace.

★ The name Colombia comes from the name Christopher Columbus.

★ Over 3,000 species of butterflies can be found in Colombia.

Did you KNOW?

This young girl became a leader in her community.

David Talks with God

Based on THE BOOK OF PSALMS

The Bible describes King David as a man after God's own heart. That means that David loved God and wanted to please Him with all he said and did. David also talked to God in prayer a lot, and many of his prayers are written down in the book of Psalms.

David begged God's forgiveness for his sins in Psalm 51: "Turn your face from my sins. Wipe out all my guilt. Create in me a pure heart, God. Make my spirit right again" (verses 9–10 ICB).

David also praised God for all the wonderful gifts He gives: "I will give thanks to you, LORD, with all my heart; I will tell of all your wonderful deeds" (9:1).

David had been a shepherd, and he knew that God was protecting him the way a shepherd protects his sheep. So David prayed, "Lord, you are my shield. You are my wonderful God who gives me courage" (3:3 ICB).

One of the most famous psalms David wrote is Psalm 23. In this one he says that the Lord is his shepherd and describes a shepherd's care: "He makes me lie down in green pastures, he leads me beside quiet waters. . . . Even though I walk through the darkest valley, I will fear no evil, for you are with me" (verses 2, 4).

David knew he could always trust God to take care of him. David said, "I will praise you, Lord, among the nations; I will sing of you among the peoples. For great is your love, reaching to the heavens; your faithfulness reaches to the skies" (57:9–10).

God wants to hear your prayers
because He loves you! You can
ask Him for help, protection,
and guidance.

He will answer because He
is your Shepherd and He
takes good care of you.

The Lord Is My Shepherd

For many years, Motlalepula's favorite place has been church, where he can worship and praise God. In fact, he has been a member of his church since he was only ten years old. He also loves to go to the Christian Commitment Club, where he has learned to deal with the hard things in his life by first asking God for help.

When Motlalepula was only six years old, his parents died, and he was sent to live with his grandmother in the southern part of the African country of Lesotho. There, he met lots of other boys and girls who were also orphans. After they finished elementary school, many of them didn't have enough money to go to high school, so they spent their days doing bad things and getting into trouble. Motlalepula was sometimes tempted to join them, but he was able to say no when they asked him to go along.

Reading God's Word and praying helped Motlalepula be strong: "Prayer helps me put God above all else. I now know that He is the Provider, and Psalm 23 is my strength whenever I feel challenged."

Motlalepula has also shared with his friends what he has learned from the Bible: "I want to help them see the importance of turning to God for solutions."

Just as David knew that he could trust God to help him, Motlalepula has learned that God cares about him too.

"I trust in the Word of God," said Motlalepula, an orphan.

Did you KNOW?

★ In the center of the national flag of Lesotho is a picture of a big black hat!

★ Lesotho is an *enclave*, meaning a country that is completely surrounded by another country—in this case, South Africa.

Lesotho teenagers learn about God.

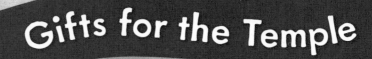

Gifts for the Temple

Based on **1 CHRONICLES 29**

David told the people, "My son Solomon has a big job ahead of him. It isn't going to be easy, but this wonderful building project he will oversee isn't for man. It's for God, so it must be the best."

Generosity means giving not just the extra of what you have, but giving even some of what you might need yourself.

The Hebrew people had always worshipped God in a tent that could be taken down and moved as they moved. But David wanted to construct a magnificent building, a holy temple for worshipping God. It would be a permanent place where people could gather to worship Him and where holy objects like the ark of the covenant could be kept. King Solomon—one of David's sons—would build the temple and decorate it with gold and silver and jewels. But where would Solomon get all the materials he needed to build such a wonderful temple? He would get them from the people!

And King David led his people by example: "I have a lot of wealth, and I'm giving it to be used in the temple. I'm giving gold, silver, bronze, iron, and wood. I'm also giving onyx, turquoise, precious gems, fine stone, and marble. I'm not giving just a little of these things but a lot of them."

David gave from the wealth of the nation, but he also gave his personal money and possessions. He showed the people what it was like to be generous when he gladly gave what he had to God. Because the Hebrew people saw David be generous, they were generous too. They happily gave gifts of gold, silver, and jewels for Solomon to use in building God's temple.

And we give generously when we give with a happy attitude.

Being Helped—and Helping Others

If almost everything you had—your clothes, your toys, your house—was destroyed by a big storm, what would you do? Would you take what you had left and give it away? That's what the children of Brock Elementary School did. In 2005, the town of Slidell, Louisiana, was hit by Hurricane Katrina, a giant storm that nearly destroyed the elementary school.

Classrooms were a mess! Papers were soaked and covered with mud. Fallen branches had broken most of the windows. It took two years to repair the damage. To help, friends from World Vision "adopted" Brock Elementary. They gave the teachers needed supplies to help the children learn. Children received backpacks full of pencils and paper and crayons.

When Christmas came, the kindergarten teacher at Brock had an idea: Why not help the children share with others in need from the kindness they had been shown? Even though these boys and girls at Brock Elementary didn't have a lot, they could still make a difference in someone else's life. So the teacher told them about the World Vision Gift Catalog, full of useful items they could donate to help others. The children were excited to use their snack money to buy a pig for a needy family. The next year they bought chickens, ducks, and goats.

Several years have passed, but the children continue to donate their snack money to help others. Martina, who still has the backpack she received after Hurricane Katrina, said, "We all love to help and support other people. Everyone thought it was good to help after we'd been helped so much."

After living through a scary storm, this class wanted to help other kids in need.

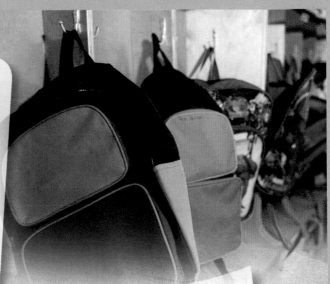

Did you KNOW?

★ Hurricane Katrina was the second strongest hurricane ever recorded in the U.S.

★ Slidell, Louisiana, sits on the edge of Lake Pontchartrain, one of the largest wetlands in the world.

A Woman Shares Food with Elijah

Based on **1 KINGS 17**

Excuse me," the prophet Elijah said to a woman who was gathering sticks for a fire. "Would you please give me a glass of water?" The woman headed for her house to get him some water. Then Elijah added, "Oh, could I have some bread too?"

God had taken good care of Elijah during the drought. There had been no rain in the land for a long time, so rivers were going dry and crops were dying. But God had told Elijah to camp by a little creek that still had some water, and He had sent birds to take food to Elijah. But then the creek dried up too. What was Elijah going to do? God told him to go to the town of Zarephath because God had ordered a woman there to give him food.

"I'm sorry. I don't have enough to share with you," the woman said sadly. "I was picking up sticks to build a fire so I could make one tiny loaf of bread for my son and me. It won't be much because I only have a little oil and flour left. After that, we will just wait to die."

"Don't be afraid," Elijah said. "Go home and do what you planned, but first make a small loaf of bread for me. Bring it to me, and then go back and make some for you and your son. This is what God says: 'The flour will not be used up, and the oil will not run out until it rains again in this land.'"

The woman went home and did exactly what Elijah had said. She made bread for him, and then she made more for her and her son. To the woman's amazement, there was enough oil in the jug and flour in the jar to make bread every day—just as Elijah had told her!

The woman learned to share even what little she had.

God will take care of His children who are generous.

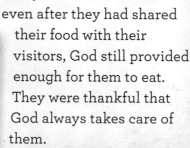

KENYA

Sharing in Faith

Have you ever been really hungry? Imagine if all you had to eat all day long was one very small bowl of soup. Then imagine that visitors came to see you, and they were hungry too. Would you share your soup with them? That's what Ekomol's family did.

Ekomol and her family live in Kenya. They are animal herders who go from place to place in search of food for their animals. At one time they had 312 goats, 38 camels, and 10 donkeys, but almost all of them were stolen. There is very little food for them to eat, but when visitors arrive, they happily share what they have with them.

One day, Ekomol's daughter-in-law was busy making porridge out of corn and soybeans. Her little girl, Kamaret, could hardly wait for it to be done.

"I want the porridge," Kamaret told her grandmother, Ekomol.

"It is very hot," her grandmother warned.

"Just bring it, and I will eat it slowly," Kamaret promised.

But when the porridge was finally finished cooking, Christian friends visiting their home received the first steaming hot bowls. Kamaret's family had not eaten for several days, but they still wanted to share.

When they finally had their turn to eat, Kamaret and her sisters, Ekidor and Lowasa, sang songs praising God. They were thankful that even after they had shared their food with their visitors, God still provided enough for them to eat. They were thankful that God always takes care of them.

These sisters live in a very dry land where food is scarce.

Did you KNOW?

★ Kenya is home to lions, leopards, buffalo, elephants, rhinoceroses, giraffes, zebras, and many other wild animals.

★ The men of the Embu tribe of Kenya dress in long black coats and white masks and are famous for dancing on stilts.

A Little Girl Makes a Difference

Based on 2 KINGS 5

If only my master could see the Lord's prophet. The prophet could cure him of his leprosy!" the young servant girl told her mistress.

Naaman, her master, was the commander of an army that had won many battles. He was an important man, but he had a terrible skin disease called leprosy. People with this disease had to leave their homes and live in camps far away from other people.

Naaman listened to the servant girl's idea and went to see Elisha, the Lord's prophet. When Naaman got to Elisha's house, a servant met him with this message: "Elisha says you should go to the Jordan River and wash yourself seven times. Then you will be healed."

Naaman was angry that a servant had been sent to deliver Elisha's message. "The prophet himself doesn't come out to see me? No! I won't wash in the river. Besides, is that river any better than the rivers at home?" He turned around and started to leave.

"Master, wait!" Naaman's servant said. "If the prophet had told you to do something difficult, wouldn't you have done it? Why not just wash and be cleaned?"

This time Naaman listened. He went to the Jordan River and washed seven times. When he came up out of the water, his skin was clean and healthy. His leprosy was gone!

Naaman went back to Elisha and said, "Now I know that there is no God in all the world except in Israel!"

Naaman was healed
because he listened to the
advice of a young girl.
God can use anyone of
any age to do His work.

A Young Boy's Important Message

Growing up in Senzani, Malawi, Edward Thomson was a happy little boy. He went to school, where he learned to read and speak English. He played soccer. He worked on the village farm, where families grew red beans, corn, sweet potatoes, and peanuts. Then a terrible disease came to Edward's country, and people started to die, including many of his family members and friends. Today people can take medicines to keep from dying of this disease, but at that time nothing could make them well.

After his aunt died, Edward wrote a poem about his feelings. A visitor to his village took a video of him reciting his poem, and that video was seen all over the United States. Edward was only seven years old, but what he said made people pay attention to what was happening in his country and throughout Africa. And people started to do something to help.

God used a young girl to give good advice to Naaman when he was very sick. And God used young Edward to tell people about what was happening to the sick people in his country.

Edward's poem was even published in a book.

Did you KNOW?

★ Malawi is called the "Warm Heart of Africa" because the people who live there are so friendly!

★ Lake Malawi is the third largest lake in Africa. It is sometimes called the Calendar Lake because it is 365 miles long and 52 miles wide.

True Worship

Based on **ISAIAH 58**

The Lord told Isaiah, "Shout loudly! Don't hold back! Tell the people about the wrong things they have done against Me so they will come looking for Me and do what is right."

Isaiah was a prophet, and God had given him the job of encouraging the Israelite people to obey God and live in a way that honored Him. Many of the people pretended to be very close to God. They acted as if they were obeying Him, but they really weren't.

Isaiah challenged them: "You are being fake! You're pretending to worship, but you are only pleasing yourselves and fighting with each other. You're not fooling God, and you aren't really worshipping Him."

Isaiah continued sharing God's message and told the people what true worship is: "God wants you to share food with those who are hungry. It pleases Him when you give homeless people a place to stay and find clothing for people who don't have any. Pay attention to the men and women, the boys and girls, around you. Help them whenever you can.

"If you help people who are in need and give your time and energy to doing whatever you can for them, your fasting and prayers will mean something to God. He will help you and guide you. God will take care of you and provide what you need. Be careful to keep God's day holy. Don't just do whatever you want to do and dishonor God. Find your joy in the Lord, and He will bless you!"

Real worship comes from the heart. Serving God by helping others is part of worship.

Worshipping Heart, Sharing Heart

Thirteen-year-old Anele loved school. Seventh grade had been the best year ever. Next year he would join the older students at a new school. Anele was a good student, so he wasn't worried that classes would be too difficult, but the new school was five miles away! Would he have enough time in the morning to fetch water from the village well for his family and still get to school on time? Would he have enough energy to walk so far on an empty stomach? Anele had a loving grandmother who worked hard to make a good home for him, but they were poor, and life in Zimbabwe was difficult.

Then a family in the United States heard Anele's story and decided to help. This family knew from reading the Bible that God wanted them to share with others the blessings He had given them to enjoy. And they knew that helping those in need was one way they could show their love for God.

They began sending money to buy food and other things that Anele needed. Thanks to these generous Christian friends, he received a bicycle so he could ride the five miles to school each day. He also got a wheelbarrow to carry water in, rather than carrying it in a bucket on his head. Because of the kindness of people he had never met, Anele's life became much easier.

Anele's new friends know that worshipping God means more than going to church on Sundays. It also means helping people who have less and caring for the needs of children like Anele.

★ The largest man-made lake in the world by volume, Lake Kariba, is in Zimbabwe.

★ The name Zimbabwe means "Great House of Stone" in the Shona language.

★ Zimbabwe was once called Rhodesia, named for South African businessman Cecil Rhodes.

Anele said the friend who helped him is "God's person."

Jonah and the Big Fish

Based on JONAH 1–3

"Jonah," God said, "I have a job for you. Go to Nineveh. Tell the people there to obey Me. Go now!"

Jonah got moving . . . but in the opposite direction of Nineveh!

Jonah lived in Israel, and he didn't like the people of Nineveh. They were Israel's enemies. So Jonah hopped on a boat and headed as far away from Nineveh as he could get!

Not long after the boat sailed from shore, a powerful storm began. Water splashed into the boat, and the waves tossed it up and down. The sailors were terrified! They threw cargo overboard to make the boat lighter.

The sailors thought Jonah might be the reason for the storm. They woke him up and asked, "Is this storm happening because of something you did?"

"Yes," Jonah said. "It's because I am running away from God. He told me to do something, and I disobeyed. Throw me overboard, and the storm will stop."

The sailors didn't want to throw Jonah into the sea, but finally they did and the storm stopped immediately. Then God sent a big fish to swallow Jonah! For three days and three nights, Jonah was inside the fish. He prayed, "God, I know I disobeyed You. Give me another chance, and I will do what You say." So God told the fish to spit Jonah up on the shore.

A seaweed-covered, soggy Jonah went right to Nineveh and told the people that they should start obeying God. They did, and God forgave them for disobeying Him!

God wanted the people of Nineveh to hear about Him. It didn't matter that they weren't from Israel; it didn't matter that they were different from Jonah.

God wants all people to know how much He loves them.

Clean Water for All

Have you ever seen one of those puzzles where you pick out the differences between two nearly identical pictures? At first glance, they look the same, but when you look closely, you realize they are very different. That's what four small villages in Ghana were like.

In some ways, the people living in the four villages were a lot alike, but in other ways they were different. They all wore the same kind of clothes, ate the same kind of food, and lived in similar homes. All of them were also very thirsty. There was no clean water in any of the villages. When people wanted a drink, they had to walk a long way to a muddy pond, where they'd fill up a bucket with dirty water that made them sick.

But one day, some World Vision friends came with the news that they could help drill wells so the villagers would always have clean water nearby. The people were very excited, and when the wells were finished, they threw a big party. The chiefs of the first three villages got up and gave speeches thanking their new friends for helping them get clean water. When the fourth chief got up, he also thanked them for helping his village get water, but then he said something else: "You are Christians, and the people in the other three villages are also Christians. The people in our village are not, but that did not stop you from giving us water. Because you have been so kind to us, we want to know more about your God."

The fourth village was different from the other three. But God loved the people of that village just as much as He loved the people in the other villages.

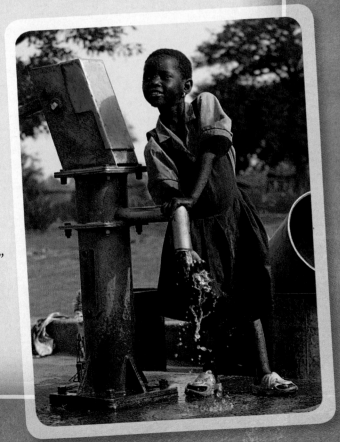

Did you KNOW?

★ Ghana is famous for its traditional kente cloth, sometimes called "the cloth of kings."

★ Over 900 species of butterflies call Ghana home, including the African giant swallowtail, which measures nearly eight inches across. It's the size of a small bird!

★ Children in Ghana attend kindergarten for two years before continuing their education.

Clean water brings life in Ghana.

Shadrach, Meshach, and Abednego knew that God would be with them no matter what—and He will always be with you too.

Shadrach, Meschach, and Abednego

Based on **DANIEL 3**

Everyone must bow and worship the king's statue! Those who don't will be thrown into a blazing furnace!" The king's messenger made this announcement throughout the land.

God's people had been forced to leave their home. They now lived in Babylon under the rule of King Nebuchadnezzar. His rules did not line up with God's rules, but people obeyed them anyway! All the people bowed down before the king's statue—everyone except Shadrach, Meshach, and Abednego. These young Jewish men refused to worship anyone other than God.

"Hey!" some men tattled to the king. "Those three refuse to bow down to your statue."

The king was furious and commanded his men to bring Shadrach, Meshach, and Abednego before him. "Is it true," he demanded, "that you refuse to bow to my statue? Don't you know that you will be thrown into a blazing hot furnace if you don't?"

"You can throw us into the furnace," Shadrach and his friends answered. "Our God may save us—but even if He doesn't, we will never worship your gods or bow down to your golden statue. We worship only the Lord God."

"Make the furnace seven times hotter!" the king shouted. The furnace was so hot that the soldiers who threw in the three men were killed. Then the king jumped to his feet in amazement. "Didn't we throw three men into the fire? Why do I see four? And the fourth man looks like the Son of God!"

Then the king yelled, "Servants of the Most High God, Shadrach, Meshach, and Abednego, come out! Praise be to your God who rescued you!"

The young men were not hurt, and they didn't even smell like smoke! God protected them because they honored Him.

God Rescues Daniel

Based on DANIEL 6

The royal administrators were grouchy. They had a problem they didn't know how to fix. Daniel, King Darius's favorite, was about to be promoted to the job that they wanted!

Daniel was not from Babylon, but he had shown that he was honest and did the right thing. King Darius had already given him an important job, and now he was about to put Daniel in charge of the whole kingdom. The royal administrators and the king's other helpers were jealous. They looked for ways to get Daniel in trouble, but he was so honest that nothing worked.

Finally they came up with a mean plan. "O King, make a law that no one can pray to anyone except you for thirty days. Any person who breaks this law should be thrown into the lions' den." These men knew that Daniel prayed to God every day, and they made their idea sound so good that King Darius signed the law.

As he always had, Daniel kept praying to God three times a day. When the men saw Daniel kneel and pray by his window, they raced to tell the king. "Daniel broke the law. He prayed to his God. He must be punished!"

The king was very sad. He didn't want Daniel thrown into the lions' den. "May your God protect you," the king told Daniel. Then Daniel was locked up inside the den full of huge, hungry lions.

The king was so worried that he didn't sleep all night. Early the next morning, he raced out to the lions' den. "Daniel, servant of the living God! Did your God protect you?" the king called out.

"My God sent His angel to keep the lions' mouths closed," Daniel answered. "I was not hurt!"

King Darius was very happy that Daniel was safe. "I command that everyone should honor Daniel's God!"

106

God rescued Daniel from danger because Daniel honored Him. God protects His children.

Protected by God's Love

Ten-year-old Hannah doesn't remember much about that terrible day in Mauritania. She was riding in the car with her father when a man began shooting a gun. The next thing she knew, she woke up in a hospital in France, where doctors and nurses were caring for her wounds. It took a long time for Hannah to get better, but once she was well, she and her family decided to return to Mauritania so her father could continue his work helping poor people.

Everyone in Mauritania was surprised. They thought their country was the last place Hannah would want to live. But Hannah's father explained that the family had come back because they loved Jesus and Jesus wants His followers to love others.

The man who shot Hannah was in prison, and Hannah wanted to see him. She wanted to tell him that, just as Jesus had forgiven her sins, she had forgiven this man for what he had done to her. Even though Bible reading is against the law in Mauritania, when Hannah and her parents visited the prison, Hannah's mom read to the man from her Bible. But instead of being arrested, Hannah and her family appeared in the newspaper, with details of their story. Even the president of Mauritania heard about them.

When Hannah's family first arrived in Mauritania, they had prayed that God would help them show His love to their new neighbors. They had no idea it would be so dangerous, but God was still with them. The people of Mauritania still remember Hannah and her family and their message of God's love.

Hannah has grown up telling her story of survival and forgiveness.

Did you KNOW?

★ If you fly over Mauritania in an airplane, you can see what looks like a giant bull's-eye. Called the "Eye of Africa," it was once thought to be the result of a meteor strike, but no one actually knows what caused it.

★ Mauritania has one of the longest trains in the world, measuring over a mile and a half long.

God gave Esther courage to do the right thing even when it was dangerous.

Queen Esther Saves Her People

Based on THE BOOK OF ESTHER

Beautiful Esther had been chosen from all the girls in the kingdom to be the new queen. The king thought she was wonderful.

But now Esther was in big trouble.

At the request of an evil man named Haman, the king had just signed a law that ordered all the Jews to be killed. And although the king didn't know it, Queen Esther was Jewish!

Esther's cousin Mordecai came to her with an important message: "You must save your people. Maybe this is the reason you became queen!"

"Have the people pray for me," the young queen responded, "and I will go to the king, even though I might be killed."

It was against the law for Queen Esther to go to the king without being invited by him, but she bravely dared to break the law and went to see the king.

She breathed a sigh of relief when the king was happy to see her. "What can I do for you, my queen?" he asked. Esther invited the king and Haman to come for dinner that night and the next night too. When they had finished eating on the second night, Esther asked the king for a big favor. "Please save me and my people. We are to be killed!"

"Who would dare do this?" asked the king.

"It is this wicked Haman! He is going to kill all the Jews, including me! I'm Jewish!"

The king was so angry that he had Haman killed instead—and the Jews were saved!

God-Given Courage

I'm very sorry," the doctor told Susan's mother. "We have bad news. Your daughter is very sick."

Susan was so sick that the doctor didn't think he could do anything to make her well. But he decided to try some new medicine, and to everyone's surprise, Susan began to get better. Her disease didn't go away, but Susan could leave the hospital and go home to be with her two little children in the village of Chibundi, Zambia.

Still, some of Susan's neighbors worried that her disease would spread to others, so they didn't want her to come home. They even started saying hurtful things about her that made her very sad. So Susan started to pray. And the more she prayed, the more convinced she was that God wanted her to start speaking out about her illness and helping others who were sick.

But speaking out took a lot of courage. The first time she went to a church to talk about being sick, Susan was scared. She was afraid people might chase her away. But they didn't. Instead, they listened carefully to what she said. Then Susan took classes to learn how to help others who were sick. "I didn't know that my work as a caregiver would impact many lives." But it really did. Now people thank Susan for helping them stay alive.

Like Queen Esther, Susan was afraid to speak out at first. But God helped her to be brave, and many people's lives were made better because of Susan's courage.

Susan feels God's love, even in her illness.

★ The name Zambia comes from the Zambezi River. Zambezi is from a local word *yambeji*, meaning "big waters."

★ Victoria Falls, named for England's Queen Victoria, is one the seven natural wonders of the world. Africans call it *Musi-o-Tunya*, meaning the "smoke that thunders."

Did you KNOW?

Working Together to Rebuild a Wall

Based on **NEHEMIAH 1–6**

Nehemiah was an important servant to King Artaxerxes of Persia. One day, Nehemiah was very sad when he went to the king. "What's wrong, Nehemiah?" Artaxerxes asked.

"I'm sad because Jerusalem, the home of my ancestors, has been burned and the wall around it has crumbled to the ground," Nehemiah answered.

"What would you like me to do?"

"Let me go there and rebuild the wall," Nehemiah said.

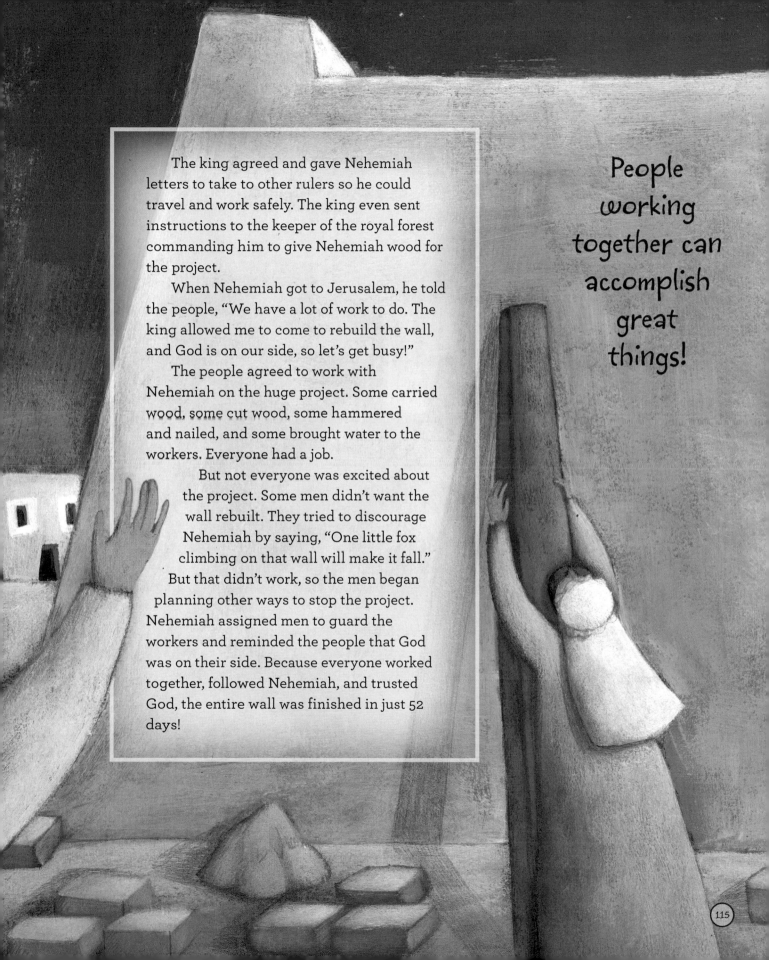

The king agreed and gave Nehemiah letters to take to other rulers so he could travel and work safely. The king even sent instructions to the keeper of the royal forest commanding him to give Nehemiah wood for the project.

When Nehemiah got to Jerusalem, he told the people, "We have a lot of work to do. The king allowed me to come to rebuild the wall, and God is on our side, so let's get busy!"

The people agreed to work with Nehemiah on the huge project. Some carried wood, some cut wood, some hammered and nailed, and some brought water to the workers. Everyone had a job.

But not everyone was excited about the project. Some men didn't want the wall rebuilt. They tried to discourage Nehemiah by saying, "One little fox climbing on that wall will make it fall." But that didn't work, so the men began planning other ways to stop the project. Nehemiah assigned men to guard the workers and reminded the people that God was on their side. Because everyone worked together, followed Nehemiah, and trusted God, the entire wall was finished in just 52 days!

People working together can accomplish great things!

Building Together

The hut that twelve-year-old George had built for his younger brother and sister in the village of Senzani, Malawi, was not very strong. After all, what did a young boy know about building houses?

But George's parents had died, and George needed to take care of his brother and sister. So when termites ate away at the family hut, it was up to George to rebuild it. Then, when he was sixteen, the termites began eating the new hut! Once again, George had to rebuild, but this time it was easier. George didn't have to do all the work alone. He had help: Christian friends saw how hard the task was for George and his brother and sister, so they all pitched in.

Nehemiah couldn't rebuild the wall around the city of Jerusalem by himself. He needed help. George needed help with a building project too. He was glad that he had helpers who were willing to work with him. Together, they could build a stronger new hut, one that would hopefully last for a long time.

George and his brother play checkers outside their home.

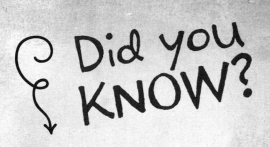

Did you KNOW?

★ Malawian women wear skirts, never pants, in their villages—and those skirts must cover their knees.

★ Lake Malawi has more than 3,000 different kinds of fish, which is more than any other lake in the world.

Malachi's Great Test

Based on THE BOOK OF MALACHI

R eturn to Me, and I will return to you," God told the people of Israel.
What is God talking about? they wondered.
"You are robbing me!" the Lord said.
How were they doing that?
Everything we have comes from God, and He wants us to use what we have—our time, our money, our talents—to give Him honor. But the people in Malachi's time thought they deserved God's blessings even though they didn't honor Him.
"Bring to Me your tithe, one-tenth of everything you earn or gain. Bring your very best to honor Me, and I will bless you! Test Me in this! Obey Me—and then watch as I throw open the gates of heaven and pour out so many blessings on you that you won't have room for them all!"

God has called His people to give one-tenth of all they have. Giving your best to God honors Him. It also provides for people who need help. And God promises to bless you when you obey.

Gifts That Honor God

Evelyn could not stop worrying! What was she going to do? It was terrible enough that her husband had died, but how would she be able to care for her three small children? She had never had a job outside her home in the Philippines, and she didn't know of any way to earn money to support her family. But then some Christian friends gave her a cow, the answer to Evelyn's prayers! Owning a cow meant she would have milk for her children, and when the cow gave birth to a calf, Evelyn would be able to sell the calf and have money to take care of her family's other needs.

But when the first calf was born, Evelyn did not keep it for herself. The people who had originally given Evelyn the cow had explained to her how much it pleases God when we share with others what He has given us. So rather than keep the calf for herself or sell it and keep the money, she gave that first calf to another family in her town that also needed help. When her cow gave birth to a second calf, she gave that one to her daughter. Finally, she made plans to sell the third calf so she could use the money to make repairs on her home.

Evelyn was faithful: she shared with other people what God had given her. And God was faithful: He provided for Evelyn's needs. Now she no longer worries about taking care of her family. Her cow is a reminder to her that God loves her and will take care of her!

Evelyn with her precious cows.

Did you KNOW?

★ The Philippines is made up of more than 7,107 islands, but only about one-third of those islands have people living on them.

★ There are more than 300 volcanoes on the islands of the Philippines, although only about 20 are still active.

New Testament

When God has unexpected
plans for us, we should try
to respond like Mary and say,
"I am Your servant, Lord God!
Help me obey You!"

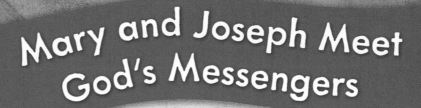

Mary and Joseph Meet God's Messengers

Based on MATTHEW 1; LUKE 1

Greetings, Mary. Don't be afraid."

Mary gasped. Who was there? And what was that bright light?

It was the angel Gabriel! "God is happy with you," Gabriel explained. "He has chosen you to do something very special. You are going to have a baby. This child will be the Son of God, and you shall name Him Jesus. God will make Him King over all things. He will reign forever."

Mary was engaged to marry a man named Joseph, so this message was very confusing. "How can any of this happen? How can I have a baby? I'm not even married yet."

"The Holy Spirit will come over you, Mary, because this baby will be God's Son," Gabriel said. "And listen to this news. Your relative Elizabeth is also going to have a baby, even though she is very old. Remember, nothing is impossible with God."

After listening quietly to all that Gabriel said, Mary responded simply: "I am God's servant. Let everything happen just as you have said." After that, Gabriel left.

When Joseph found out that Mary was going to have a baby, he thought about canceling their wedding. He didn't know that the baby was God's Son—until God sent an angel to talk to him. "Joseph, don't cancel your wedding. The baby that Mary is carrying is God's Son! And when He is born, name Him Jesus, because He will save His people."

A Baby Named John

Based on LUKE 1

Mary went to visit her cousin Elizabeth, and sure enough, the older woman was having a baby! Elizabeth and her husband, Zechariah, had never had children, so it was a big surprise when one day an angel visited Zechariah with a message from God. The angel was Gabriel—the same angel who had visited Mary.

"God knows that you and Elizabeth have always wanted children. Now you will have a child. Name him John. God has a special job for him. He will tell people that God's Son is coming," the angel said.

Zechariah questioned Gabriel's news. "Are you sure? How can this be?"

"Because you did not believe me," Gabriel said, "you will not be able to speak until the baby is born." And Zechariah's voice was gone!

The moment Mary greeted Elizabeth, Elizabeth's baby jumped inside of her. Elizabeth's baby seemed to know that Mary's baby was Someone very special!

For nine long months, Zechariah was unable to speak. When the baby was born, family members suggested different names for him. But Zechariah wrote on a tablet, "His name is John." Immediately his voice came back because he had obeyed God!

God has a plan for every single one of us, even before we are born.

God planned for Jesus and John the Baptist to show the world His love, and He wants each one of us to show others His love too!

God's Big Plans for a Little Boy

Have you ever thought about what you want to be when you grow up?

When Titus was a little boy, he might have imagined becoming a teacher or a police officer or a doctor. He never would have dreamed that someday he would be the assistant attorney general for the whole country of Bangladesh. After all, his family was poor, and they lived in the out-of-the-way village of Joyramkura. The war for independence had ended, but it was still a struggle to survive. That's why Christians from all over the world had gone to Bangladesh to help. They had taken food and had built schools, bridges, and even the hospital where Titus was born.

When Titus was old enough to go to school, these same Christians gave him books, school supplies, and shoes. After Titus finished high school, they helped him become a lawyer. Titus wanted to help people who had been treated unfairly, whose land had been stolen, or who had been put in jail for something they didn't do. Titus eventually became the assistant attorney general of Bangladesh, one of the most important leaders in his whole country.

Throughout Titus's life, Christians showed God's love for him, and they helped him see that God had plans for him, plans to do good and to help others. Just as God had important work for Jesus and John the Baptist to do, He had important work for Titus, and He has important work for you!

Helped as a boy to go to school, Titus now has a very important job.

128

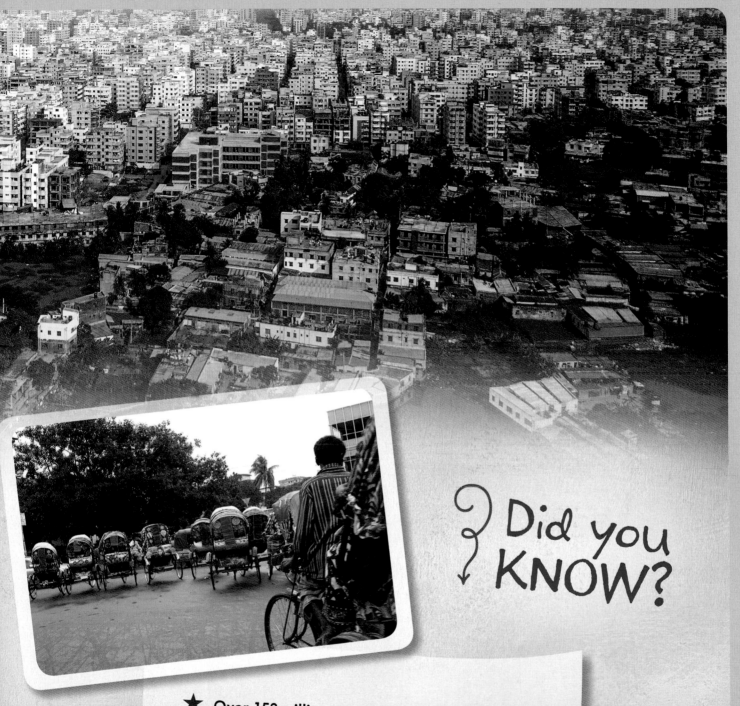

? Did you KNOW?

★ Over 158 million people live in Bangladesh, making it the most crowded country in the world.

★ Instead of cars, people travel in rickshaw tricycles.

Jesus Is Born

Based on LUKE 2

Clip-clop. Clip-clop. The little donkey slowly made its way down the road. Mary bounced along on the donkey's back, and Joseph walked beside her. They were on their way to Bethlehem to be counted in the Roman census. The king wanted to know how many people lived in his kingdom, so he had ordered people to return to the towns where their ancestors had lived. Joseph's ancestor, David, had come from Bethlehem, so that's where Joseph and Mary were going.

Mary clutched her belly and moaned a bit as she bounced along. The baby would be born any day now. Riding on a donkey wasn't very comfortable. She couldn't wait to get to Bethlehem so she could rest. But when she and Joseph finally arrived, they found the little town crowded with people. Not one room was available anywhere.

At last they met a kind innkeeper who offered to let them stay in his stable. And that very night, Baby Jesus was born. Mary lovingly wrapped her little boy in strips of cloth and laid Him down to sleep in a manger.

What a gift! God gave everyone in the world the greatest gift anyone could ever imagine—His own Son, who would save us from our sins.

God sent His Son, Jesus, as a gift to the world because He loves all people so much—including you!

Another Humble Beginning

Born in a stable and placed in a manger—that was a very humble starting point for the Lord and Savior, Jesus. Even today, people are born into humble settings. Moses Pulei, for instance, grew up in a mud hut in Namanga, Kenya.

As a boy, one of his chores was to take care of his family's sheep. It was a big job, and his father didn't think he had time to go to school *and* do his chores too. But Moses' mother wanted him to learn, so when he was eight years old, he began attending the primary school in his village. When Moses was old enough to go to high school, he had to run barefoot many miles each way to get to school. He must have been very tired when he got home!

Moses was a member of the Maasai tribe in Kenya and grew up in a family that did not worship Jesus. But when Moses was in 12th grade, he went to a camp run by some Christians. They explained that God loved people so much that He came to earth as a baby named Jesus, born in a stable in Bethlehem. They also told Moses that God invites everyone who loves Jesus to be part of His family. Moses was very happy to hear this good news. He wanted to know more about God's love for Him and about Jesus. Soon Moses loved Jesus too.

From Africa all the way to the U.S.—Moses as a college student.

★ Maasai men and women pierce and stretch their earlobes and also wear large metal hoops at the tops of their ears.

★ Maasai women and children shave their heads. Maasai men wear their hair in long braids dyed with red clay.

★ Maasai homes are called Inkajijik. The women are in charge of building them using sticks, grass, mud, and cow dung.

Did you KNOW?

The shepherds worshipped Jesus when they saw Him. That's what happens when people meet Jesus. Worship fills their hearts, and praises fill the air!

Good News!

Based on **LUKE 2**

It was a quiet night. Stars were twinkling in the velvety black sky. In the fields outside of Bethlehem, sheep were settling in for the night while their shepherds watched over them.

Suddenly, an angel appeared in the dark sky above the fields—and the shepherds were terrified! But the angel said, "Don't be afraid. I have great news for you that will make people everywhere very happy! Tonight a baby was born in Bethlehem. He is Christ the Lord! You will find this baby wrapped in strips of cloth and lying in a manger."

At that exact moment, the entire sky was filled with a choir of angels. Now the frightened shepherds were totally amazed! The angels praised God: "Glory to God in the highest and on earth peace to all men!"

Then, just as suddenly as they had come, the angels disappeared. The sky was dark and night was quiet again. The shepherds looked at one another, trying to understand this incredible experience. Suddenly, one of them said, "Let's go into Bethlehem and find the new baby!"

The shepherds found Mary, Joseph, and the baby in a stable, just as the angel had told them. The shepherds were so excited that, after they left the little family, they told everyone they saw about the new baby and what the angel had said about Him! Then the shepherds went back to their fields, praising God for everything they had heard and seen.

God Guides the Wise Men

Based on **MATTHEW 2**

"Look! What an amazing star!" The men from the east were stunned. There in the sky was the biggest, brightest star they had ever seen. It sparkled like a diamond in the black night sky. These wise men knew what the star meant: a new King had been born in a land far away from them. Wanting to meet the King and worship Him, they packed up gifts for Him—gold, frankincense, and myrrh—and started the journey to find Him.

The star guided them on their way. When they got to Jerusalem, the men asked people in the city if anyone knew where they could find the King.

People from all countries and people of all nationalities can worship Jesus. The Bible says that one day every knee will bow to Him. On that day, the whole world will know about His love!

Herod, the king of Judah, heard about the wise men and the baby they were searching for. His chief priests and teachers knew that the Scriptures said the King of the Jews would be born in Bethlehem. So Herod sent for the wise men. "When you find this new King," Herod said, "let me know where He is so that I may worship Him too." But King Herod didn't really want to worship the newborn King. Herod wanted to kill Him! He didn't want any new King taking over his kingdom.

The wise men continued following the star until they finally found Jesus. These men from a faraway country gave their gifts to Jesus, and they bowed and worshipped Him. Then, because God had warned them in a dream not to return to King Herod, they returned home a different way.

It's hard to leave your home and live in a place where everything is different. But sometimes, because of danger, war, or famine, people have to leave their homeland. They are called refugees.

Joseph, Mary, and Jesus were refugees in Egypt.

Run to Egypt!

Based on MATTHEW 2

"Get up, Joseph! Get up! Now!"

What? Who's waking me up in the middle of the night? thought a sleepy Joseph.

"Joseph, you and Mary need to take Jesus to Egypt. You have to leave because Herod wants to hurt your baby. So hurry! Leave right now! And don't return to Israel until I tell you it's safe." An angel was giving Joseph a very important message.

Wide awake now, Joseph knew he had to get going. He woke Mary, she bundled up Baby Jesus for the chilly nighttime journey, and the little family left for Egypt.

King Herod had become very angry and afraid when the wise men arrived in Jerusalem looking for the new King. Herod didn't want anyone taking over his kingdom! So this bad king ordered his soldiers to kill all the baby boys in and around Bethlehem who were two years old and younger. It was a very sad time.

Mary, Joseph, and Jesus made it safely to Egypt and stayed there until the angel visited Joseph again. "King Herod is dead," the angel reported, "and it's safe for you to go back to Israel."

Mary and Joseph were glad to be able to go back to their own country, but they didn't return to Bethlehem. They went to Nazareth, where they had lived before Jesus was born. They were happy to be home.

Fleeing to Safety

Back at home in Somalia, Isnino Siyat had lived in a hut made of mud and cow dung. It was strong. But in Dadaab, the refugee camp in Kenya, Isnino worried about her new home. It was just a tent made out of scraps of cloth and sticks she found on the ground. It looked like it might fall down any minute.

Isnino had no tools to build a proper home. Because of fighting in her country, she and her husband had been forced to leave quickly, taking with them nothing except their two little babies. Isnino wasn't strong enough to carry the things she might need to start a new life in Kenya, but she had no choice but to leave her homeland. The rains had stopped coming. Some people said it was the worst drought in 60 years. Isnino had no way to feed her children. Her only hope was to get to the refugee camp.

Now Isnino has help from new Christian friends who are making sure that refugee families like hers have what they need to survive. They are passing out cooking supplies, water, and even Plumpy'nut®, a peanut butter–like food that the children really like. And Plumpy'nut® is good for them too!

Joseph, Mary, and Jesus had to leave their home and live for a while as refugees in Egypt. But God protected them, and one day they were able to return to their home.

Isnino hopes that one day she and her family will also be able to go home. But until then she is glad for help from her new Christian friends.

Isnino and her children live in a small hut and hope for help.

★ Two of the gifts the wise men gave to the Baby Jesus—myrrh and frankincense—can be found in Somalia.

★ Somalia is located on a piece of land that, because of its shape, is known as the Horn of Africa.

John the Baptist

Based on MATTHEW 3

Big, tasty locusts! Sweet, sticky honey! *Soooooooo good*, John thought to himself as he ate his lunch.

John the Baptist wasn't like most people. He lived in the desert. He wore clothes made of camel hair. He ate locusts and honey. And he told as many people as he could that Jesus was coming!

John also told crowds of people to stop doing bad things and to start obeying God. Then, when people were sorry for their sins and wanted to obey God, John baptized them in the Jordan River. John also explained to these people that he baptized with water but that Someone was coming who would baptize them with the Holy Spirit and guide them to live in a way that pleases God. John was talking about Jesus!

One day, Jesus Himself went to the Jordan River and asked John to baptize Him. John couldn't believe that Jesus—God's Son—wanted to be baptized by him!

So Jesus and John walked into the water, and John baptized Him. When Jesus came up out of the water, the heavens opened and the Spirit of God came down in the shape of a dove.

Speaking from heaven, God's big voice said, "This is My dear Son, whom I love, and I am very happy with Him."

John knew that Jesus was God's Son and that his job was to help people get ready to know Jesus.

Sharing the Good News

Roth Ourng was nervous. Why had these visitors come to his little village in Cambodia? He had watched them set up a hospital and had seen them working with the farmers in their fields. But why?

Finally, Roth got up the courage to ask. The visitors told him, "We are followers of Jesus Christ, and He wants us to show love to our neighbors."

"Who is this Jesus?" Roth wanted to know. The visitors gave Roth a Bible in his own language and took him to meet a Cambodian pastor living in another village. The pastor explained that God loved Roth so much that He sent Jesus to earth to die for his sins. The pastor also told Roth that God wanted him to become part of God's family.

Roth was very excited and immediately invited Jesus to become his Savior. But Roth didn't keep this good news to himself. He told all his friends about Jesus! Now Roth is a pastor who shares God's love with his entire village. Each week, over 80 Cambodian Christians worship God together.

Just as God used John the Baptist to help people get ready to know Jesus, God used those Christian visitors in Roth's village to help him get ready to know Jesus. And then Roth shared what he had learned about Jesus with others.

Pastor Roth is a **joyful servant of God.**

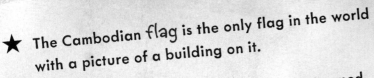
★ The Cambodian flag is the only flag in the world with a picture of a building on it.

★ Rice is very popular in Cambodia. It is steamed, fried, and made into noodles. It is even served as a dessert with fruit.

★ Every November, Cambodians celebrate *Bon Om Touk*, the Cambodian Water Festival, with rowing races on the Mekong River.

Jesus Chooses Twelve Helpers

Based on MATTHEW 4; MARK 2; LUKE 6

Have you ever gone fishing?

Jesus' friends Peter and Andrew were fishermen. Every day, they
went out on their boat and threw their nets into the Sea of Galilee to
catch some fish.

Fishing was Peter and Andrew's job, but Jesus had something better
to offer them. "Peter! Andrew!" He called to them. "Come and follow

The people Jesus called to be His special helpers were just regular people. They were not religious leaders or teachers. God uses all kinds of people to do His work!

Me, and I will make you fishers of men." Both men immediately dropped their fishing nets and went with Jesus.

Two other fishermen, James and John, were sitting in a boat helping their father repair their fishing nets when Jesus called their names. Like Peter and Andrew, James and John left their boat right away and followed Jesus. Now four fishermen were following Jesus.

Jesus called eight more men to follow Him. Their names were Matthew, Philip, Bartholomew, Thomas, James, Simon, Judas, and Judas Iscariot.

Fishermen, tax collectors, and other ordinary men were doing their ordinary jobs until Jesus called their name. When He did, they knew that the most important thing they could ever do was to follow Jesus. So when Jesus called these people, they stopped what they were doing and followed Him.

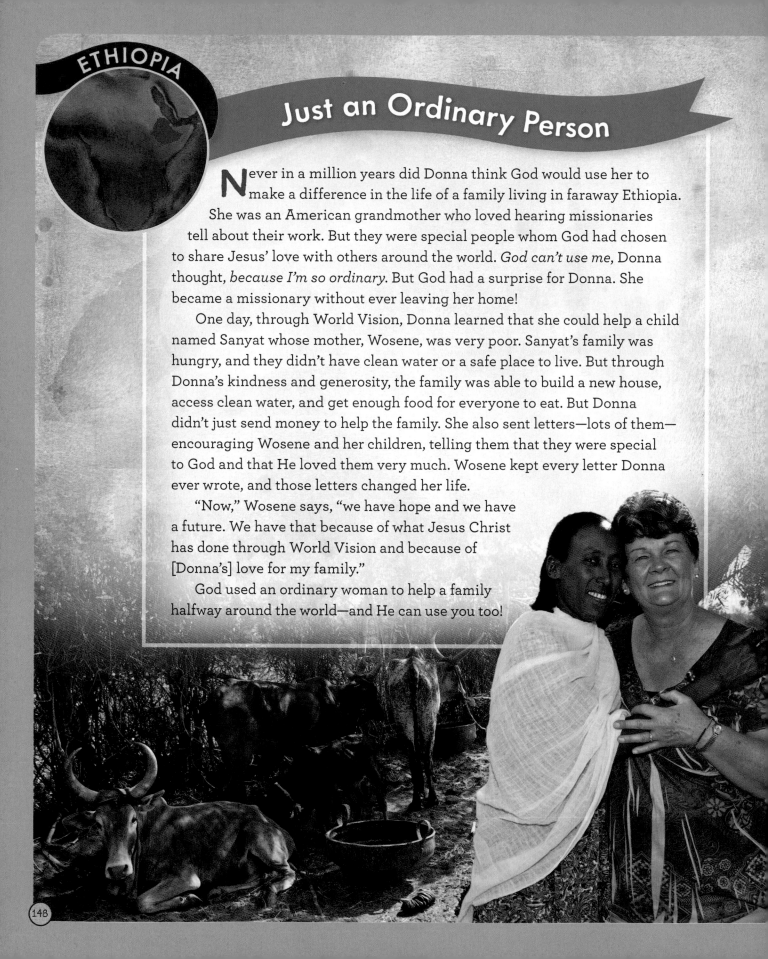

Just an Ordinary Person

Never in a million years did Donna think God would use her to make a difference in the life of a family living in faraway Ethiopia. She was an American grandmother who loved hearing missionaries tell about their work. But they were special people whom God had chosen to share Jesus' love with others around the world. *God can't use me*, Donna thought, *because I'm so ordinary*. But God had a surprise for Donna. She became a missionary without ever leaving her home!

One day, through World Vision, Donna learned that she could help a child named Sanyat whose mother, Wosene, was very poor. Sanyat's family was hungry, and they didn't have clean water or a safe place to live. But through Donna's kindness and generosity, the family was able to build a new house, access clean water, and get enough food for everyone to eat. But Donna didn't just send money to help the family. She also sent letters—lots of them—encouraging Wosene and her children, telling them that they were special to God and that He loved them very much. Wosene kept every letter Donna ever wrote, and those letters changed her life.

"Now," Wosene says, "we have hope and we have a future. We have that because of what Jesus Christ has done through World Vision and because of [Donna's] love for my family."

God used an ordinary woman to help a family halfway around the world—and He can use you too!

★ Ethiopia is the birthplace of coffee.

★ The Ethiopian calendar has 13 months in it.

★ In Ethiopia, parents and children don't share the same last name. Children use their father's first name as their last name.

Did you KNOW?

Donna sent letters and love to Wosene's family before they got to meet.

Lost Sheep, Lost Coins, and Lost People

Based on LUKE 15

Why does Jesus spend so much time with tax collectors?" the religious leaders muttered. "They cheat people. They're totally dishonest. If Jesus wants people to believe what He teaches about God, why does He hang out with people who do bad things? Why doesn't He spend time with better people—like us?"

To help the religious leaders understand why He spent time with people who did bad things, Jesus told them some stories. "What would you do if you were a shepherd who had 100 sheep and one of your sheep got lost? Would you leave the 99 sheep alone and go looking for that one lost sheep? That's what a true shepherd does because he cares about every single sheep. And when the shepherd finds that one lost sheep, he calls all of his friends to celebrate with him!"

Jesus also told this story: "Suppose a woman has ten silver coins but loses one of them. She still has nine coins left, but the tenth coin is important too. So she searches everywhere for it. She lights all the lamps, sweeps the floor, and looks until she finds it. And when she finds the coin, she calls her friends and asks them to celebrate with her."

Then Jesus said, "The shepherd and the woman celebrated when they found what they had lost. When I find someone, like a dishonest tax collector who realizes he is lost and chooses to follow Me, the angels in heaven celebrate. Whenever a person stops sinning and turns to God, He rejoices too."

Everyone on the planet is important to Jesus. He celebrates whenever a person chooses to follow Him.

God's Dearly Loved Child

Like children everywhere, most Indian children go to school when they're young, but Nagavani's family was too poor to send her to school. So for as long as she could remember, eleven-year-old Nagavani had worked in a matchbox factory. Her daily job was to fill 1,444 tiny paper boxes with matches.

Nagavani liked to look out the window as she was counting matches. Every day she saw boys and girls walking to school, laughing, playing, and having fun. It made her sad because she wanted to do those things too. Watching the smiling, happy children, she wondered, *Do I have to work in the matchbox factory because I'm not as good as other children? Or maybe God does not love me as much as He loves them?* When a Christian visitor came to Nagavani's village, she thought this might be her chance to find out. So she listened carefully when her mother asked the visitor, "Why are you here? And what do you see when you look at us?"

The visitor explained that when she looked at Nagavani, she saw a little girl just like those children Nagavani watched through the window of the matchbox factory. But more important than what the visitor saw was what God saw when He looked at Nagavani: He saw His dearly loved child. If Nagavani had been the only person on earth, God still would have sent His Son, Jesus, to show her just how much He loved her and to invite her to become part of God's family!

Thanks to her Christian friends, Nagavani no longer has to work in the matchbox factory.

Did you KNOW?

★ The game of chess was invented in India.

★ There are more post offices in India than anywhere else in the world.

★ India's Hindi-language movie industry, called Bollywood, is the world's largest maker of movies.

The Prodigal Son

Based on LUKE 15

"I want my money now!" demanded the younger brother. "I want to have parties and be with my friends. I don't want any rules. So give me everything I would get after you die. I want it now!"

Heartbroken, the father gave his son the money, and the boy left home. He went far away and wasted it all. When his money ran out, his friends ran off. He had to get a job feeding pigs—and he was so hungry that even the pigs' food looked good enough to eat!

Finally the boy realized he didn't need to live like that. "Back home, my father's workers have food to eat, and I'm starving to death. I'll go home and tell Dad that I know I've sinned. I'm not worthy to be treated like his son, but maybe he'll let me work for him."

The boy was still far from home when his father saw him coming. This very happy father ran to his son and gave him the biggest hug ever! "Father," the boy said, "I've sinned against you. I'm not worthy to be treated like your son. I am so sorry."

But his father was already telling the servants to get food ready for a party. "My son is home with me again. He was lost, but now he is found. Let's celebrate!'"

Jesus told this story to show how God responds when people ask Him to forgive their sins. Like a father waiting for a rebellious child to return, God wants us to return to Him, and He welcomes us home when we do.

God is like a wonderful, loving Father who welcomes us home when we return to Him.

A Father's Love

Do you ever think about all the things your parents do for you? Because they love you, they want you to have everything you need to grow up into happy, healthy adults: a warm home, plenty of food to eat, and clothes to wear. They also want to teach you about right and wrong and how to be kind and loving to others.

But sometimes parents aren't around to give their children what they need. When Johnny was only seven years old, he was living alone on the streets of a little town in Bolivia. His mother had died, and he didn't have anywhere to go or anyone to take care of him. So he started hanging out with some bigger boys who were always getting into trouble. Soon Johnny was in trouble too. And when Johnny got older, it only got worse.

Then one day a pastor told Johnny that he needed to change. He told Johnny that Jesus loved him and wanted him to put Jesus first in his life. "And so," Johnny said, "I took his advice, and since then I am no longer like I used to be."

Just like the father in the Bible who was so happy when his runaway son returned to him, Johnny's heavenly Father is happy that Johnny turned his life around and came to Him. Because of his heavenly Father's love, Johnny is a new and different person.

With God's help, Johnny became a happy family man.

Did you KNOW?

★ The Uyuni Salt Bed in southwest Bolivia is the world's largest salt flat.

★ La Paz, the capital of Bolivia, located high in the Andes Mountains, is the highest capital city in the world.

157

We don't know the name of the boy who shared his food, but he teaches us an important lesson. He gave Jesus what he had and then watched Jesus do an amazing miracle. You never know what God will do with what you give Him!

Jesus Feeds 5,000 People

Based on MATTHEW 14; MARK 6; LUKE 9; JOHN 6

Look at all these people! There are thousands!" one of the disciples said. News of Jesus' amazing miracles and wonderful teaching had spread, and now crowds of people followed Him everywhere. As He often did, that afternoon Jesus had been healing the sick and then began to teach. The people listened for a long time.

Soon it would be time for dinner. The disciples went to Jesus. "Master, it's getting late. Send the people into town so they can buy food."

They were surprised when Jesus said, "You give them something to eat."

"A person would have to work more than eight months to have enough money to feed them all!" one of Jesus' disciples pointed out.

"I'll share my food," a young boy said. "I don't have much, only five small loaves of bread and two small fish, but you can have it."

After the disciples got all the people to sit down, Jesus took the boy's bread and fish and thanked God for it. Then He broke the food into pieces and gave the pieces to His disciples to pass out to the people. With just five small loaves of bread and two little fish, Jesus fed more than 5,000 people—and there were leftovers!

Sharing the Little They Had

Can you imagine what it would be like to live in a house without a door, a floor, or any windows? Now imagine what it would be like to live in that house when snow was on the ground. That's what it was like for Mr. and Mrs. Rostas and their five children during the winter months in a little village near Cluj, Romania.

Their World Vision sponsors sent money to help them buy what the family needed. One year, the Rostas family used that money to buy a door and windows. The next year, they used it to put in a floor.

Another year, when Mr. and Mrs. Rostas received money from their sponsors, they decided to give some of it to the other children in their village whose families were also very poor. Every child received a gift because Mr. and Mrs. Rostas shared the little they had with others.

When these Christian friends sent money to Mr. and Mrs. Rostas, they had no idea that so many people would be helped. But they were glad to learn that God had used their small gift to help more people than they had ever imagined. These Christian friends shared what they had, then Mr. and Mrs. Rostas shared what they had, and God turned it into enough for everyone!

- ★ There are nearly **200** castles in Romania.

- ★ The traditional sport of Romania is oină, which is similar to baseball.

- ★ Romania is the only European country where the brown bear still lives in the forest.

Cracked windows do little to protect children from extreme cold in Romania.

The Wedding Banquet

Based on MATTHEW 22

"Come to the feast! The king is waiting!" the royal servant called as he went from door to door. The king had planned a big banquet to celebrate his son's wedding. Now that the food was prepared and everything was ready, the king sent out his servants to gather the guests who had been invited.

But none of the guests wanted to come. They all had excuses and chose not to go to the party.

When the king heard about it, he told his servants, "Go to the street corners. Invite anyone and everyone you find."

That's what the servants did. It didn't matter who the people were, where they came from, what their jobs were, what they looked like, or how much money they had. The king welcomed anyone who wanted to join him. Soon the banquet hall was filled with guests who were happy to celebrate with the king—and the people who had been invited first would have been very surprised to see who was there!

God invites everyone to be part of His family, even people you might not expect!

163

An Unexpected Welcome

There are certain jobs children should never, ever have, and one of those jobs is being a soldier. But in some places in the world, entire armies are made up mostly of young boys. One of those places was Northern Uganda. That's where Michael and Joseph grew up.

One day, when Michael and Joseph were out playing with friends, grown-up soldiers came and forced them to join their army. The boys didn't want to go, but they had no choice. Michael and Joseph were very sad about the things the grown-up soldiers made them do in the army, and they escaped as soon as they could. The boys found their way to the Children of War Center, where Christian friends were helping other children who had escaped from the army.

When Michael and Joseph arrived, they were very afraid. What would happen when these people found out they had been in the army? Would they be angry? Would they punish the boys? Imagine Michael's and Joseph's surprise when a big crowd rushed over to greet them.

Instead of being angry with the boys, these new Christian friends were smiling and singing and welcoming them in. Then they took Michael and Joseph into the chapel, where they continued to sing and worship God, thanking Him for bringing the boys safely home. The boys learned that nothing they had done could keep God from loving them. And they saw that God wants everyone to be in His family.

God loves and cares for all His children, and He wants all of them—including *you*—to know Him and love Him. Just like the king who invited everyone to join him at the wedding feast, God invites everyone to join His family. Have you said "Yes" to God's invitation?

Learning to play again at the Children of War Center.

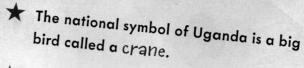

★ The national symbol of Uganda is a big bird called a crane.

★ One-third of all people in Uganda have cell phones!

★ Matooke, a dish made out of plantains, is many Ugandans' favorite meal.

Did you KNOW?

In chapel, Michael and Joseph began to feel God's love and mercy.

When God calls you to do something, you don't need to be afraid. He will help you and protect you. He is always with you—and nothing is stronger than He is!

Walking on Water!

Based on MATTHEW 14

It was a windy night at sea. Huge waves crashed against the little boat the disciples were in!

Whoosh! Splash!

"Harder! Row harder!" The disciples strained to get to shore. They were afraid the powerful winds and rough waters would sink their boat and they would all drown.

As if the storm wasn't frightening enough, the disciples then thought they saw a ghost. Someone or something was walking on the water, and the disciples were terrified.

"Don't be afraid! It's Me!" the Man on the water called. The disciples knew that voice. It was Jesus!

"Lord, if it's really You," Peter shouted back, "tell me to come to You!"

"Come!" Jesus answered. Peter leaped out of the boat and started walking on top of the water toward Jesus. But when Peter realized what he was doing, he took his eyes off Jesus, looked down at the waves crashing against his knees . . . and started to sink!

"Lord, save me!" Peter cried. Immediately Jesus reached out and caught him.

"Why did you doubt?" Jesus asked Peter as they climbed into the boat.

As soon as they were in the boat, the wind died down. The disciples said, "This man is truly God's Son." And they began to worship Jesus.

No Need to Be Afraid

It was quiet and dark as Lily and her two younger sisters walked down the dirt road. At night, a group of men with guns had come into villages like the one Lily's family lived in, so her parents had sent Lily, Harriet, and Nancy to the Noah's Ark Children's Center in Gulu, Northern Uganda, where they would be safe.

Every morning at six-thirty, after sleeping at the center, Lily and her sisters would leave the shelter and walk to school, where Lily studied chemistry, math, and English. Then, at the end of the day, she would walk her sisters back to their village, where they washed up, ate a small dinner, and visited with their parents. When it was almost dark, the girls would walk back to Gulu and the Noah's Ark Center.

Lily's mother was so glad that her two youngest daughters had their big sister to look after them on the long walk into town. At night, they could count on their big sister to tuck them in, read them a story, and help them not be frightened. But who helped Lily? Jesus did. Lily knew that Jesus was always with her. Even when she felt very alone, she knew He was there to help her.

Jesus reminded Peter and the disciples not to be afraid because He was with them. Lily was certain that Jesus was with her too so she didn't have to be afraid.

Children sleeping at the Noah's Ark Children's Center.

At sunrise, the children of Noah's Ark Center dash off to school.

★ Of the only 786 mountain gorillas left in the world, about half of them live in Uganda.

★ Bicycle and motorcycle taxis are called *boda-bodas*.

★ Because of its natural beauty, Uganda is known as the "Pearl of Africa."

DID YOU KNOW?

The Good Samaritan Helps His Neighbor

Based on **LUKE 10**

"Jesus, God's Word tells me that I am to love my neighbor, but who is my neighbor?" a man asked. Jesus answered by telling this story:

Traveling this dangerous road makes me nervous, the man thought. *But so far, so good.* Just then, robbers grabbed him, beat him up, stole everything he had, and left him half dead on the road.

A priest came walking by, but when he saw the wounded man, he crossed the road and kept going.

Then a temple worker came along the road. "Oh my," the temple worker said. "You're in a bad way, but I have to get to a meeting. No time. No time." He stepped over the hurt man and kept going.

Later another man, a Samaritan, came upon the severely injured man. But unlike the first two men, the Samaritan stopped. He was kind. He cleaned and bandaged the man's wounds. He put the man on his donkey, took him to an inn, and paid the innkeeper to take care of him.

Jesus told this story to teach that we are to be kind and help *anyone* who needs help, not just the people who live next door.

Anyone who needs help is your neighbor, and you can show Jesus' love by helping that person.

Helping Our Neighbors

What would you do if you saw a child hurt on the playground and nobody else was around to help? Would you stop to see what you could do? Would you find a grown-up who could help?

When the good Samaritan found a wounded traveler lying on the side of the road, he took time to care for the injured man. In the Democratic Republic of the Congo, a woman named Mama Masika found a little baby lying hurt in the bushes in a town called Ufamando, and she also stopped to help.

War has been going on in the Democratic Republic of the Congo for as long as most people can remember, and many children have lost their parents because of the fighting. One of those children is Baby Espoir, whose name means "hope." But his life didn't start out very hopeful.

One day, after the fighting in her village had ended, Mama Masika went through the bushes looking for people who needed help. That's when she heard a baby's cries and found little Espoir. He was very sick, so Mama Masika hired a bicycle taxi to take her and Espoir the 89 miles to the Minova Hospital.

In addition to Espoir, Mama Masika now cares for seven other children who also lost their parents in the war. And she is encouraging her neighbors to do the same. She leads a group of women who, all together, have adopted 40 orphaned children. She and her friends are being good Samaritans to their neighbors who need help and who need to know the love of Jesus that Mama Masika brings.

Mama Masika **takes good care of the children in her village.**

Did you KNOW?

★ Natural resources like copper, cobalt, gold, coltan, tin, and zinc—which are used in making cell phones and computers—can all be found in the Democratic Republic of the Congo.

★ In 2002, Mount Nyiragongo erupted and poured a river of lava approximately 200–1,100 yards wide and up to two yards deep through parts of the city of Goma.

Jesus spent His time on earth doing God's work. When we help others, we are doing God's work too.

174

Jesus Heals a Man Born Blind

***Based on* JOHN 9**

A blind man sat begging by the side of the road. One of the disciples turned to Jesus and asked, "Why was this man born blind? Was it punishment because he sinned or because his parents sinned?"

"Neither," Jesus answered. "The man is blind so that people can see God's power at work in his life."

Jesus knelt down, spit on the dusty ground, and made some mud. Then He rubbed the mud on the blind man's eyes. "Now go wash your face in the Pool of Siloam," Jesus said to the man. The man did exactly what Jesus told him to do, and when he washed the mud off his face, he could see!

People who had known the man his whole life were confused. "Is this the same man who used to beg for money?" Some thought it was, but others said, "No. It's just someone who looks a lot like him."

"No! I *am* the one who had to beg!" the man said.

"But now you can see?" the neighbors asked.

"I don't know how Jesus healed me. I just know that I was blind, but now I can see."

Jesus Heals a Paralyzed Man

Based on MARK 2

Excuse us! Please! Excuse us! Please let us through!"
Four men wanted to carry their friend into the crowded house where Jesus was. Their friend couldn't walk, but the four knew that Jesus could heal him if they could just get him close enough.

The friends suddenly had an idea. They went up on the roof of the house and began to cut a hole right over the room where Jesus was teaching. Then the four men slowly lowered their paralyzed friend down until he was right in front of Jesus!

Jesus looked up at the four friends who were peering through the hole they had made and saw that they believed He could make their friend walk. Then Jesus turned to the paralyzed man and said, "Son, your sins are forgiven."

This made the religious leaders angry! "Who does He think He is? Does He really think He has the power to forgive sins?" they shouted.

"What is easier to say: 'Your sins are forgiven,' or, 'Get up and walk'?" Jesus asked. "The Son of Man has the authority to forgive sins." Then turning back to the paralyzed man, Jesus said, "Get up, take your mat, and go home."

The man jumped to his feet and left the house, praising God!

Four men took their crippled friend to Jesus, and he was healed. Do you have a friend you can bring to Jesus? Is there someone you can encourage and help today?

Jesus Heals a Man with Leprosy

Based on **MATTHEW 8**

All day long, Jesus had been teaching people how to live in a way that would make God happy. As Jesus came down from the mountainside where He had been teaching, a large crowd of people followed Him. But that big crowd didn't prevent one particular man from approaching Jesus and kneeling at His feet.

It was clear from the sores on his body that he was very sick. He had a terrible skin disease called leprosy and was supposed to stay away from other people so they wouldn't get it too.

Jesus was willing to help people no one else would help. Do you know someone who is sick or lonely or needs a friend?

"Lord, if You want to," the man said, "I know You can make me well!"

Jesus knew that people never got close to lepers. But because He loved the sick man, Jesus reached out His hand and gently touched him. The man hadn't been touched for a long time, and the touch of Jesus' hand felt good to the sick man's heart.

Then Jesus said, "I do want to help you. Be clean."

Immediately, the man's skin was clear of all the sores. He was completely healed—blessed not only to have clean skin but also to know Jesus' love!

In the same way that Jesus reached out to the man with leprosy, you can reach out to help others in need.

Helping When No One Else Will

Maheshwari could not even remember the last time someone had touched her. Everyone was too afraid they would get sick, just like Maheshwari was. Even her family was afraid they would catch her disease. When Maheshwari begged her family to let her move back in with them in their little house in Chennai, India, they made her sleep outside on the back porch. Once, she fell down and cried out, but her mother was so fearful that she would not help her up. That made Maheshwari so sad.

Then a World Vision helper came to see Maheshwari. Right away he bent down to help her. To his surprise, she began to cry, but not because she was sick. She cried tears of happiness because it was the first time in so long that someone had cared about her enough to touch her. This Christian friend helped Maheshwari stand up and then took her to the doctor. Now she is much better. She is so thankful to be well again that she takes care of other women who are still sick. Helping others is the way she thanks Jesus for making her well.

A healthy **Maheshwari** shopping in the market.

Did you KNOW?

★ India has the highest bridge in the world. It is called *Bailey Bridge* and is located in Ladakh between the Dras and Suru rivers in the Himalayas.

★ The language spoken by most people in India is called *Hindi*.

★ *Cows*, goats, and even elephants wander through the city streets right next to cars!

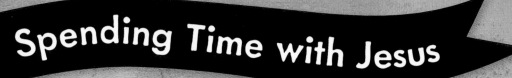

Spending Time with Jesus

Based on **LUKE 10**

"So much to do!" Martha grumbled to herself. She rushed around the kitchen, chopping, stirring, and preparing food. She wanted this meal to be perfect for Jesus and His friends. Martha cooked and cooked and worked and worked. It wasn't easy to make dinner for that many people! *Why isn't Mary in here helping me?* Martha thought her sister should be in the kitchen with her. *What is she doing?*

Martha could hear Jesus' voice in the next room, and when she peeked around the corner, she saw Mary sitting right at Jesus' feet, listening to everything He said. Now fuming mad, Martha stomped back into the kitchen and angrily stirred her big pot of soup.

Finally, Martha marched into the other room. "Jesus, don't You care that I'm doing all this work by myself? Tell Mary to help me with dinner!"

"Martha, Martha," Jesus sighed. "You are worried about things that aren't that important. Mary has chosen the most important thing—being with Me."

The best thing you can do with your time is give it to Jesus. He loves when His children spend time with Him.

Zacchaeus was not the sort of person others expected Jesus to spend time with. But when Jesus reached out to Zacchaeus, his life and the lives of many others were changed.

Zacchaeus

Based on LUKE 19

Excuse me! . . . Please move . . . I can't see!" The short man Zacchaeus hopped and pushed and peeked through the crowd, trying to see Jesus. "Aha! Here is the answer!" Zacchaeus saw a sycamore tree, ran to it, and climbed up on a sturdy branch. *Now I can see Jesus when He walks by,* he thought.

Zacchaeus was a tax collector, and no one liked tax collectors because they charged too much money and cheated people.

"There He is!" someone yelled. "That's Jesus!"

Zacchaeus looked down the road, and right in the middle of the crowd was the Teacher named Jesus.

Jesus walked in front of the sycamore tree where Zacchaeus was sitting and stopped. Jesus looked up at the little tax collector and said, "Zacchaeus, come down. I am coming to your house today." Zacchaeus scrambled down from the tree as fast as he could.

"He's going to be the guest of a *sinner*?" people muttered to themselves. The religious leaders thought they deserved a visit from Jesus much more than a cheating tax collector did.

But Zacchaeus was sorry for the wrong things he had done. "Lord, I will give half of everything I own to the poor. And I will pay back everyone I cheated four times what I owe them!"

"Salvation has come to this house today," Jesus said. "I have come to find people like you who need to know God."

The Woman at the Well

Based on JOHN 4

The hot sun burned through the sky as the Samaritan woman trudged up to the well. With tired feet and aching arms, she carried buckets to fill with water.

As she dipped the first bucket into the well, she heard a warm and gentle voice.

"May I have a drink of water?"

The man's request startled her. First, why was a man sitting by the well in the middle of the day? Second, in Bible times, men didn't ask women for help. And third, this man was a Jew—and Jews hated Samaritans because the Samaritans didn't obey all of God's laws.

"Why would You ask me for a drink of water?" the surprised woman asked.

"If you knew who I am, you would ask Me for water," Jesus answered. "People who drink this water from the

Jesus loves everyone, even people others wouldn't consider good enough to talk to—and He offers Living Water to all of us.

well will get thirsty again, but whoever drinks the water I have will never be thirsty again."

As she continued to talk with Jesus, the Samaritan woman realized she had never spoken to anyone like Him. In fact, she realized she had met the Messiah, so she ran to town and told everyone she knew about this surprising conversation and this amazing Man.

Praying for Water

When you get a drink of water or take a bath or brush your teeth, do you ever think about where the water comes from? Rakia knows exactly where her family's water comes from. Very early every morning, she walks to a muddy pond outside her village in Niger. There she stands knee-deep beside animals that come to drink, bathe, and cool themselves in the dirty water. Then Rakia lowers her yellow bucket down into the pond and fills it with just enough water for her family to use that day. Her two-year-old sister, Faouzia, is very sick, and her mother, Zeinabou, knows that her baby's illness is caused by drinking such dirty water, but they don't have any choice.

Unlike Zeinabou's family, the Samaritan woman whom Jesus met at the well had clean water to drink. What she needed was the Living Water that comes from knowing Jesus as Lord and Savior. Zeinabou and her daughters need both clean water and Living Water. And you can help!

When you drink a cold, clean glass of water, will you pray for the people around the world who drink only water filled with dirt and bugs and diseases? When you take a bath, will you remember to pray for children who will never wash in anything but a muddy pond? And as you pray for their need for clean water, will you also ask God to give them the Living Water that only Jesus brings?

Even without enough clean water, Zeinabou does the best she can for Faouzia and her family.

Did you KNOW?

★ Most childhood diseases around the world are related to water, hygiene, and sanitation.

★ Nearly half of the population of Niger doesn't have clean water.

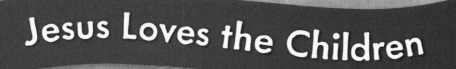
Jesus Loves the Children

Based on **MARK 10, LUKE 18**

Giggling and singing. Skipping and hopping. And did that little girl just do a cartwheel?

Happy girls and boys were going to see Jesus! Parents were carrying infants in their arms. Young children held their parents' hands tightly. Some rode on their daddies' shoulders as their parents made their way through the crowd so they could get close to Jesus. Every child was excited to see Jesus. Children love Jesus.

"Stop! Stop!" one of the disciples cried, running toward the families. "Leave the Teacher alone!"

"But we want to see Jesus. We want Him to bless our children," one father said.

"Jesus is busy now. You can't bother Him," the disciples said. "He is doing important work."

But when Jesus heard what His disciples were saying, He stopped them. "Let the little children come to Me. Don't stop them. They can teach you adults how to trust Me and believe what I say. Only people who believe the way these children do will enter My kingdom."

So the disciples stepped aside and watched the Teacher. Jesus looked at every child with smiling eyes and blessed each boy and girl who had come to see Him.

Children are important to Jesus. He cares about every single child in this very big world.

Learning from Children

Can you believe it? The children are sitting down together! After so many years of fighting between our people, how can our children work together in peace?

Thoughts like those must have gone through the minds of many Albanian and Serbian parents as they watched their children participate in the World Vision Kids for Peace Project. Ten years after the war had ended, it was still hard to imagine that this event was actually happening: 200 Serbian and Albanian children were happily working together to paint a giant rainbow and write messages about peace and love.

Their parents could hardly believe their eyes! Although the children of the village of Rubovc, Albania, attended school in the same building, the adults had separated the Albanian and Serbian children into two different classrooms. Outside, an invisible line divided the playground so that Serbian and Albanian children could not talk or play together.

Some of the bad feelings leftover from the war ran so deep that

the adults did not think peace was possible. But here, as the parents watched, children from both groups were happily playing together. They wanted to share an important message with their parents: Albanians and Serbians can live together in peace. And their parents were beginning to listen!

When the disciples tried to keep the children away from Jesus, He told them that children are important. He reminded them that grown-ups can sometimes learn a lot by watching children. That is certainly true in Rubovc, where children are setting a good example for their parents by working together for peace in their community.

Did you KNOW?

★ One-third of all the raspberries eaten in the world are grown in Serbia.

★ When people nod their heads up and down in Albania, it means *no*. When they shake their heads from side to side, it means *yes*.

In place of war, children lead the way to peace.

The Widow Gives

Based on MARK 12

"Excuse me."

"Oh, pardon me."

"Watch out! Coming through!"

The temple was loud and busy, but the woman loved this time. As she waited patiently for her turn to give her offering, she said a prayer of thanks to God for all His gifts to her. Some people might think it was a strange prayer for her. After all, she was a widow. Her husband had died, leaving her very poor. Sometimes she didn't even know where her next meal was coming from. But she still praised God for all He had given her.

Clink, clink, clink. Money jingled as people dropped it into the offering box—and some people dropped in a lot of money!

When it was her turn, the widow quietly put in two coins. Together they were hardly worth a penny. Then she bowed her head and again thanked God for taking care of her.

From across the room, Jesus saw the widow give her offering, and He looked at her with love and approval in His eyes. He said to those with Him, "This poor widow gave only two small coins, but really she gave more than all the rich people did. They gave what they did not need, but she gave everything she had."

When you give gifts to God, He is not concerned about their size or amount. He is concerned about your heart. Are you giving thankfully and generously?

Birthday Presents That Made a Difference

What is your favorite thing about your birthday? Is it inviting all of your friends and family over to your house and having a party? Maybe what you like best is eating cake and ice cream or getting lots of presents.

Just before her eleventh birthday, Kara was watching television. A news anchor was talking about a terrible earthquake that had just hit the country of Haiti, leaving many people without food or homes or hospitals to care for them. Kara lived in a part of the United States that also had earthquakes, so she understood how scared the children of Haiti must have been and how sad they now were. When she thought about them, she was sad too, so she decided to do something to help.

But what could she do? She was only a child; she didn't have a job or money of her own to send to the children of Haiti. Then she got an idea! Since her birthday party was only a few days away, she decided to ask everyone she had invited to bring something to help the children of Haiti instead of bringing a birthday present for her.

Kara

At her party, Kara collected enough to help lots of Haitian children. And she didn't miss the birthday presents at all. In fact, it felt good to know that even a young girl can make a big difference in the lives of others. "It was better for them to provide clothes and food for children in Haiti instead of getting me things I don't really need," Kara said.

★ Christopher Columbus landed on Hispaniola in 1492. He thought he had found India or Asia.

★ The nation of Haiti shares the island of Hispaniola with the country of the Dominican Republic.

Jesus Brings Lazarus Back to Life

Based on JOHN 11

Where is Jesus? Mary wondered. *We sent for Him two days ago.* Her sister, Martha, was wondering the same thing. Their brother, Lazarus, had been very sick, and they knew their friend Jesus could help him. So they had sent a messenger, but Jesus hadn't come.

By the time Jesus finally arrived in Bethany, Lazarus had died. The sisters and many friends were together in the house, sharing their sadness. But when Martha heard that Jesus was near, she rushed out to meet Him.

"Lord, why didn't You come? Our brother wouldn't have died if You had been here," Martha said to Him.

"I am the resurrection and the life. Don't you believe that everyone who believes in Me will never die?" Jesus asked.

> Jesus promised that everyone who believes in Him will live with Him forever in heaven!

200

"Yes, Lord. I believe in You."

Martha returned home to get Mary, and together the sisters went with Jesus to where Lazarus was buried. Jesus cried, sharing their sadness.

When they got to the tomb, Jesus said, "Move the stone."

"But, Jesus, Lazarus has been dead for four days," Martha said.

"Didn't I tell you that if you believed, you would see God's glory?" Jesus said.

The stone was rolled away, and Jesus looked up to heaven and said, "Father, thank You for always hearing My prayers." Then He shouted, "Lazarus, come out!"

Out of the tomb came a man wrapped in burial cloths. It was Lazarus! Jesus had raised him from the dead. Lazarus was alive again!

A Second Chance at Life

Life after the big earthquake in Haiti was difficult, but you wouldn't know it by looking at Demosi.

Always smiling, this mother of two little girls who once sold things on the side of the road in Port-au-Prince was now too busy to feel sorry for herself. Although Demosi had lost a leg and an arm when a big building fell down on top of her in the earthquake, she was not sad. She was happy that God had protected her from greater injury and that she was still able to care for her daughters. She was still able to lead the choir at church. She was still able to praise God for His faithfulness in her life.

What did Demosi most want people to know about her? "Tell them you have seen Lazarus and she is alive!" Thinking about everything that had happened to her, Demosi felt like Lazarus, who once was dead but had been made alive again in Jesus.

Just as Jesus raised Lazarus from the dead, Jesus gave Demosi a new chance to live and a new purpose for living. Instead of being a shopkeeper, she is now an encourager, helping the thousands of other people in her community who lost so much in the terrible earthquake. She shares the good news that no matter how bad things might seem, God is with them and wants to give them new life through faith in Jesus.

★ The Indian name for the country of Haiti is *Ayiti* and means "Land of High Mountains."

★ Haiti enjoys a tropical climate, and palm trees there can grow up to 60 feet tall!

Did you KNOW?

 Demosi's spirit stays strong even after a terrible earthquake.

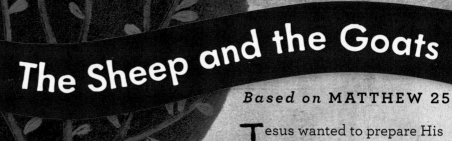

The Sheep and the Goats

Based on MATTHEW 25

Jesus wanted to prepare His followers for the end of time, so He told them about some things that will happen.

"Someday I will come back to earth from heaven, surrounded by angels. I will separate people like a shepherd separates the sheep from the goats. I will put the people who follow Me, like sheep, on My right side and the people who

When we help people in need, it is just like we are helping Jesus.

go their own way, like goats, on My left side. Then I will turn to the sheep and say, 'You are so blessed. The kingdom of God is for you. I was hungry, and you gave Me food. I was thirsty, and you gave Me a drink. I was a stranger, and you invited Me into your home. I was naked, and you gave Me something to wear. I was in prison, and you came to see Me.'

"These people will say, 'Lord, when did we do all these things?'

"I will answer, 'When you helped anyone who needed these things, you were helping Me.'

"Then I will turn to the goats on My left and say, 'Get away from Me. . . . I was hungry, but you didn't give Me food. I was thirsty, but you gave Me nothing to drink. I was a stranger, but you ignored Me. I was naked, but you didn't give Me clothing. I was in prison, but you didn't visit Me.'

"These people will ask, 'When did we see You with any of these needs and not help You?'

"I will reply, 'When you ignored anyone who needed these things, you were ignoring Me.'"

SWAZILAND

Showing People the Love of Jesus

Do you have a bicycle? Do you and your friends have fun riding around your neighborhood? Nomsa enjoys riding her bicycle too.

Nomsa is a volunteer community caregiver, and she rides her bicycle to the homes of the 124 sick patients she looks after in her village and in neighboring villages in Swaziland, the African country where she lives. She gives them medicine and food, helps them with their children, and comforts them when they are in pain. With her kindness, she shows them the love of Jesus.

Phetsile is one of Nomsa's patients, and she says that sometimes Nomsa doesn't *do* anything for her, that the two just sit and talk. But as much as any medicine, Nomsa's friendship, encouragement, and prayers are helping Phetsile get well.

A lot of people Nomsa cares for have no one else to help them. People in the community are afraid that if they visit a sick person, they might also get sick. But Nomsa is not afraid. She knows that Jesus loves every one of her 124 patients and that He has asked her to love them as well. As she rides her bicycle throughout the community, she remembers Jesus' words: when she cares for her sick parents, it is just as if she is caring for Jesus.

Did you KNOW?

★ Most Swazis eat a food made of ground corn called *mealie meal*.

★ King Mswati III has been king of Swaziland since he was only 18 years old.

 Nomsa is a caregiver and a hope-bearer.

Jesus Comes to Jerusalem

Based on LUKE 19

You'll see a young donkey when you first enter the village," Jesus told two of His disciples. "Untie the donkey and bring it to Me. If anyone asks you why you are taking it, just say that the Lord needs it, and no one will stop you."

Jesus' friends obeyed. They found the donkey, and sure enough, as they were untying it, someone asked, "Why are you taking that donkey?"

"The Lord needs it," they replied. Then they took it to Jesus, threw their coats on its back, and Jesus got on it. The strong little donkey carried Him into Jerusalem.

Crowds gathered along the way, and they began shouting, "Blessed is the King who comes in the name of the Lord! Peace in heaven and glory to God in the highest!"

People thought Jesus was such a great king that they threw their coats down on the road to honor Him. Others grabbed branches from the palm trees and waved them over Jesus as He rode by. Their shouts of worship filled the air!

The religious leaders in the crowd were upset by all the noise and praise. "Tell Your followers to be quiet!" they told Jesus.

Jesus calmly answered, "The truth is that if the people were quiet, the stones on the road would cry out in praise!"

Jesus deserves our praise because of who He is and what He has done for us. He loves to hear His children praise Him!

The Last Supper

Based on **MATTHEW 26; JOHN 13**

It was a special night for Jesus and His twelve disciples. They were together to celebrate the important holiday called Passover.

At the evening meal, Jesus stood up. He walked over to the bowl of water and picked it up. Then Jesus did the servant's job: He washed His disciples' feet. Jesus wanted them to understand that they were also to be servants who help people.

After that, as all the men were sitting around the table, Jesus said, "One of you is going to betray Me."

Each of the disciples asked Jesus, "Is it me? Am I the one who will become Your enemy?"

"The man who will be My enemy is dipping his bread into the bowl at the same time I am," Jesus said. All the disciples looked at the bowl and saw that Judas was holding a piece of bread in it.

"Is it really me?" Judas asked.

"Yes, it is you," Jesus answered.

Then Jesus thanked God for the bread that was in the center of the table, broke it into pieces, and passed it around. Jesus said, "Eat this bread, and remember that I died for you." Then He took the cup of wine, thanked God for it, and offered some to His friends. "Drink this wine, and remember My blood poured out so that your sins can be forgiven."

Jesus showed us what it looks like to be a servant when He washed His disciples' dirty, dusty feet. He even served the man who would become His enemy.

Jesus Prays

Based on **LUKE 22; JOHN 17**

Jesus knew that in a few hours He would be arrested and killed. One of the last things He did before that was very important: Jesus prayed.

"It's time, Father. Bring glory to Your Son so that I can give glory back to You."

Then Jesus prayed for His listening disciples: "Father, I have shown You to My friends, and they obey You. They know that everything I teach comes from You. These friends of Mine are Your people. I have protected them while I was here with them, but now I must leave. Father, please protect them."

Jesus also prayed for all who will believe, and that includes us! "Father, I pray that all believers will be united as You and I are united so that all people will learn that You love them."

When Jesus finished praying, He and His friends, the disciples, went out to the Mount of Olives.

One of the last things Jesus did before He died was pray. He prayed for His friends sitting with Him around the table, and He prayed for you too!

Jesus Is Arrested

Based on MATTHEW 26–27; LUKE 22–23; JOHN 18–19

Jesus knelt in the Garden of Gethsemane and prayed. He prayed so hard that His sweat was like great drops of blood falling to the ground: "Father, if there is any other way for Me to save people from their sin, let Me avoid dying on a cross and being separated from You. But I love You and these people so much, Father, that I will do whatever You want Me to do to help them."

Suddenly, Jesus heard the noise of soldiers with swords and spears coming toward Him. Jesus' disciple Judas was leading the way. Judas walked up to Jesus and kissed Him on the cheek to show the soldiers which person to arrest. The soldiers grabbed Jesus. Then one of Jesus' friends took a sword and cut off a soldier's ear.

"Stop!" Jesus cried. "Peter, put away the sword!" Jesus touched the soldier's ear, and it was instantly healed.

The soldiers took Jesus away to the high priest, who asked Him, "Are You the Christ, the Son of God?"

When Jesus said, "Yes, it is as you say," the high priest exploded in anger.

"That's it! Jesus is claiming to be God! He must be killed!"

Jesus was taken to Governor Pilate. Pilate didn't think Jesus was guilty of any crime and wanted to allow Jesus to go free. But the crowd demanded that Pilate release Barabbas, a terrible murderer, instead. "What should I do with Jesus?" Pilate asked the crowd.

"Crucify Him!" the crowd shouted. So Pilate handed Jesus over to soldiers to be killed even though He had done nothing wrong.

Jesus, the Son of God, never did anything wrong. But He died willingly to pay for the sins of all people.

Peter Denies Jesus

Based on MATTHEW 26; JOHN 18

When the soldiers took Jesus away from the Garden of Gethsemane, Peter followed along at the back of the crowd. He tried not to draw attention to himself. After the soldiers dragged Jesus into the courtyard of the high priest, Peter waited in the shadows outside to see what would happen.

Since it was a cold night, Peter went over to a fire to warm his hands. A servant girl saw him and said, "Hey, I've seen you with Jesus."

"No, you're wrong," Peter said.

A little later, someone else asked Peter, "I've seen you before. You're one of His disciples, aren't you?"

"No! I'm not!" Peter said.

Finally, one of the high priest's servants said, "I saw you with Jesus in the Garden earlier tonight."

Sometimes it's hard to be brave and tell others that you love Jesus. But even when people make fun of us or don't believe, we can know that standing up for Jesus is right!

"I don't know what you're talking about!" Peter shouted. Just then he heard a rooster crow, and he remembered what Jesus had told him: "Before the rooster crows, three times you will say you don't know Me."

Peter also remembered Jesus' warning that all of His friends would turn away from Him and that He would be alone. Peter had immediately disagreed with Him. "Everyone else may leave You, but I will never leave You!" Peter had said so confidently.

Now Peter wept bitterly. He knew that, no matter what, Jesus should always come first in our lives.

Standing Up for Jesus

When you think of someone who's very brave, do you think of superheroes like Spider-Man and Captain America, who fight bad guys and protect the world from danger? When the people of the Ansokia district in Ethiopia think of someone who's brave, they might think of Teshome Demissi.

Teshome's parents were farmers, and he grew up alongside his seven brothers and sisters, attending school and caring for the family's animals. But when Teshome was in fourth grade, rain stopped falling, and the crops his family grew began to die. There was a terrible famine. Children began leaving school because they were too hungry to pay attention. Out of 50 children in Teshome's grade, only eight were left.

Then some people from World Vision began visiting the school to pass out food for the children to eat. They talked about Jesus and sang songs about His love for them. One kind man asked Teshome if he wanted to know Jesus better. Teshome was too afraid of what his parents would think, so he said no.

Many years went by, and once again a friend from World Vision talked to Teshome about Jesus and invited him to become Jesus' follower. This time Teshome said, "Yes!" But his father was not happy. His father told Teshome that he would have to make a choice between him and Jesus. Now a grown man himself, Teshome made the courageous choice to follow Jesus!

Today Teshome tells everyone about how much Jesus loves them. His church has even asked him to work as a missionary in another village. Even when people don't believe, Teshome bravely shares the good news of Jesus' love.

With courage, Teshome shares the good news of Jesus.

? Did you KNOW?

★ *Doro wat* is a popular dish of chicken stew, and lentil stew is called *mesir wat*.

★ Ethiopia was once called Abyssinia.

★ Traditional Ethiopian homes are round huts called *tukuls*.

Jesus never sinned, but He loves people so much that He was willing to die for our sins.

Good Friday

Based on MATTHEW 27; MARK 15; LUKE 23; JOHN 19

It was the saddest day in all of history. Jesus, God's only Son, the only One who had never done anything wrong, was about to be crucified on the cross to pay for the sins of the world.

Two thieves were already hanging on crosses on the hill called Golgotha. The soldiers threw Jesus to the ground, nailed His hands and feet to the wooden cross, and lifted it so it was standing upright. Above Jesus' head they put a sign that said "King of the Jews."

People standing around the cross made fun of Jesus: "Look at the King of the Jews! Can't You save Yourself?" and "If He's God's Son, why isn't God saving Him?"

Jesus' only response was to pray: "Father, forgive them. They don't know what they are doing."

Even one of the men hanging on a cross next to Jesus made fun of Him: "Prove you're the Messiah. Save Yourself—and save us too!"

The other thief was shocked. "Aren't you afraid of God? We deserve to die for what we did, but this Man doesn't deserve to die. He hasn't done anything wrong!" Then the man looked at Jesus and said, "Please remember me when You come into Your kingdom."

"I promise you this: you will be with Me today in heaven," Jesus said.

At about noon, the sky turned dark as night, and Jesus cried out to His Father, "It is finished! Father, I give My spirit to You." Then He died.

Jesus Is Alive!

Based on **MARK 16**

Three days later was the *best* day in all of history.

Some women who were followers of Jesus sadly and quietly filled baskets with spices, oils, and perfumes for Jesus' burial. They didn't talk much as they walked toward the tomb outside of town.

"How are we going to move the big stone that's in front of the entrance to the tomb?" one woman asked. "It's too heavy for us."

They got close to the tomb, and one of the women cried out, "Look! The stone has been rolled away! The tomb is open!"

As the women rushed inside, they saw a man wearing a white robe sitting there, and the women were frightened. Jesus' body was gone!

"Don't be afraid," the man said. "I know you came looking for Jesus, who was crucified, but He is not here. He is no longer dead! He is alive again! Go tell His disciples that Jesus has risen from the dead and that He will meet them in Galilee."

What a miracle! Jesus, who died for our sins, had come back to life! The women ran back to town to tell Jesus' disciples!

Jesus' resurrection is proof of God's promise that everyone who believes in Him will live forever. Nothing is impossible for Him!

Nothing Is Impossible for God

Have you ever given up on something because it seemed impossible? Lopez felt like giving up many times growing up in Sudan. When he was only six years old, he was taken from his mother by soldiers who wanted to make him a soldier too. Put into a prison with other boys, he and three friends escaped and ran all the way to Kenya to a camp for people who had been taken from their families. Most of them were children.

Although he was frightened and lonely, Lopez was sure that God was protecting him. For ten years, he ate only one meal a day, and when he wanted to play soccer, he had to run for miles before he could take his place on the field. But that made him very fast, so fast that he dreamed of one day running in the Olympics.

Lopez loved Sunday mornings, when he could go to the camp church to worship God. One Sunday, the priest announced that 3,500 boys from the camp would be allowed to move to the United States. Lopez applied to be one of them, and he prayed that if it was what God wanted, he would be chosen. And he was! Lopez went to live with a kind family in the United States, and one day, after college, he became an Olympic runner. He was even given the honor of carrying the American flag in the opening ceremonies of the 2008 Olympic Games in Beijing.

In many ways, Lopez's story seems impossible. But nothing is impossible for God. He can turn a lost boy from Sudan into an Olympic runner, and because of Jesus' resurrection, He can give us eternal life through faith in His Son.

Lopez worked hard to train for the Olympics.

This mother, Nyibol Ring, was happy to be able to return with her children to her family's homeland in the world's newest nation, South Sudan.

Did you KNOW?

★ The Lost Boys of Sudan are a group of over 20,000 boys who were separated from their families or orphaned during the second civil war in Sudan.

★ In July 2011, the country of Sudan was divided into two independent countries: Sudan and South Sudan.

★ Before the country was divided, Sudan was the largest country by area in Africa.

A Dentist's Best Friend

We know how important it is to take good care of our teeth. Because we want our smiles to be healthy and bright, we brush and floss and visit our dentist regularly. But some children aren't able to do all of that. Children who live deep in the jungles of the Amazon rain forest, for example, don't all have toothbrushes and toothpaste, and most of them never get to see a dentist.

But that was before Dr. Joel came! Dr. Joel is a jolly dentist from Manaus, Brazil, who works on a big, white medical boat that travels up and down the Rio Negro River, docking every few miles so that children from the jungle villages can receive medical and dental care. Long lines of children and their parents wind back into the jungle as they wait patiently for their turn to go on the boat. Then, one by one, they climb into Dr. Joel's big dental chair. Most of them have never seen anything like it, so Dr. Joel jokes and laughs and tells them stories so they won't be frightened.

One of Dr. Joel's favorite stories is about his Best Friend. Dr. Joel asks each child if they have a best friend, and then he tells them about his Best Friend, Jesus, and about how much Jesus loves them. Dr. Joel uses every opportunity he has to share the good news about Jesus. He wants to make sure that no one ever leaves his dentist chair without a bright, clean smile—or without hearing that Jesus can be their Best Friend too!

Kids say "ahhh" for Dr. Joel, who serves God as he cleans teeth.

Did you KNOW?

★ The Amazon rain forest is the biggest tropical rain forest in the world.

★ Brazil is the largest Portuguese-speaking country on earth.

★ Brazil has the only team to have played in every soccer World Cup tournament, and they have the most wins—five!

The Gift of the Holy Spirit

Based on ACTS 2

Whhhhrrrrrr. Wooooossssshhhhh.

"What is that noise?" someone asked.

"It sounds like the wind blowing."

As the sound grew louder, small flames like fire began to appear above the apostles' heads. *What's happening?* people wondered.

Jesus had promised His disciples that after He went back to heaven, God would send the Holy Spirit to help them. And He did! The men were filled with God's power, and right away some of them began to speak in languages they had never before spoken. It was amazing!

All believers receive the gift of the Holy Spirit, who helps them do God's work and be more like Jesus.

Just as God had planned, people from other countries were in Jerusalem when this happened. "I hear my own language!" they cried out. "These men are from Galilee. How can they speak so we understand?" they asked one another.

Some people made fun of them. "They probably just had too much to drink."

But Peter said, "Listen, these men are not drunk. No, this is exactly what the prophet Joel said would happen: 'In the last days, God says, I will pour out My Spirit on all people.'

"You know that Jesus was here with us. He did miracles by God's power. He taught you about God. Yet some of you handed Him over to be put to death. God raised Him from the dead, and now Jesus has given us God's Holy Spirit so we have the power to do His work."

Many people listened to Peter, and that very day 3,000 repented of their sins, believed in Jesus, and were baptized.

An Amazing Miracle

Based on ACTS 3

"Come on, John!" Peter said. "We don't want to be late for afternoon prayers." They barely noticed the crippled man sitting by the temple gate. He sat there every day, begging for money from the people going to pray in the temple.

"Can you spare a few coins?" the man asked as Peter and John hurried by. They stopped and looked at the man who was holding out his hand.

"Look at us," Peter said. The man did, expecting Peter to give him some money.

Instead Peter said, "I don't have any money to give you. But I will give you what I have. In the name of Jesus Christ of Nazareth, get up and walk!"

The man didn't know what to think. Then Peter took his hand and lifted the man to his feet. The man was amazed that he could actually stand on his own! His ankles and feet were suddenly strong. He was so happy that he began jumping around and praising God! He went right into the temple with Peter and John to give thanks to God.

"Hey! Isn't that the crippled man who begs by the gate?" people asked one another. They couldn't believe he was walking around. Everyone who saw him was amazed!

We serve an amazing God who can heal a crippled man, make his legs strong, and enable him to walk—and to jump with joy.

233

God Heals

Vikas's favorite sport was soccer. What he loved most was running and kicking the ball down the field. But then the earthquake struck, and it looked like Vikas would never be able to play soccer again. Vikas was inside his house in a part of India called Gujarat when the shaking began. It happened so suddenly that Vikas did not even have time to run outside, so when the walls of his house fell down, his feet were crushed under a pile of rocks. It took a long time for villagers to rescue him, and by then the damage to his feet could not be repaired.

But one day, some Christian visitors went to Vikas's village. They saw this little boy being carried around by his mother, and they wondered if something could be done for him. They learned that, in order to walk again, Vikas needed an operation: doctors would replace his broken feet with new, artificial ones. But his mother was very poor, and she could not afford to take him to a doctor. One of the visitors had an idea. He wasn't a doctor; in fact, he didn't know anything about medicine. But he had saved some money, and he wanted to use it to help pay for Vikas's surgery.

God used a miracle to heal the crippled man Peter and John found sitting by the temple gate, and God healed Vikas by using a doctor and a Christian visitor who was willing to share what he had. Now, with his new feet, Vikas is again running and kicking a soccer ball, happy that God healed him.

Vikas stands tall on his new legs.

★ There are more than 450 languages spoken by the people of India today.

★ The children's game Chutes and Ladders, originally called Snakes and Ladders, was invented in India in the thirteenth century!

Did you KNOW?

The Disciples Spread the Word

Based on ACTS 4–5

God sent His Holy Spirit to His disciples to give them courage to share the good news of God's love and to help them know how to live in a way that pleased Him. He still does the same thing today!

Because the Holy Spirit was with them, the first followers of Jesus boldly proclaimed that Jesus was Lord, cared for those who were sick, and shared what they had with people in need. Because of what Christ's followers said and how they lived, more and more people became followers of Jesus:

The Holy Spirit helped the early Christians live in a way that showed God's love to the world.

* "Your family doesn't have enough food to eat? Well, I have more than I need. I'll share with you," one man said to another.
* "I can help you care for your sick child," a woman offered a young mother.
* "Here," said a family to the disciples. "Please take this gift. We sold our things so you can use the money to help the poor."

Just like the Holy Spirit worked in the lives of those first followers of Jesus, He works in the lives of Jesus' followers today, helping us to show God's love to the world.

A Gift of Goats

Every day after school, children go to the Brown House in Northport, Alabama. They play, get help with their homework, and learn about Jesus.

One Christmas, a volunteer at the Brown House named Andrea suggested that the children buy a goat as a present for a poor child on the other side of the world. The children at the Brown House were excited, but they didn't have any money. Andrea had an idea: they could make and sell Christmas cards. She got out some paper and felt and buttons and glue, and the children got to work. At their big Christmas party, they sold every card they had made, and to their surprise, they earned enough money to buy two goats and sponsor a child.

The next year, the Brown House kids made more cards and raised more money, this time enough money to sponsor two more children and provide them with things they need to grow up happy and healthy, things like food, water, health care, and education. The Brown House students support a little boy in Rwanda named Placide, ten-year-old Laxmi in India, and eleven-year-old Seada in Ethiopia.

The children at the Brown House learned everything they could about the places their sponsored children live and what their lives are like. Andrea thinks that loving their neighbors around the world has helped the children of the Brown House too. Now they know that even though they are young, they can make a big difference in the lives of other people by showing them Jesus' love.

Children in Alabama use what they have to help kids who have much less.

★ **Rwanda** is known as the "Land of a Thousand Hills."

★ *Gebeta* is a popular game among children in Ethiopia. It is played with seeds or pebbles and a row of cups. You may have played something similar called *mancala*.

★ The national bird of India is the peacock.

Did you KNOW?

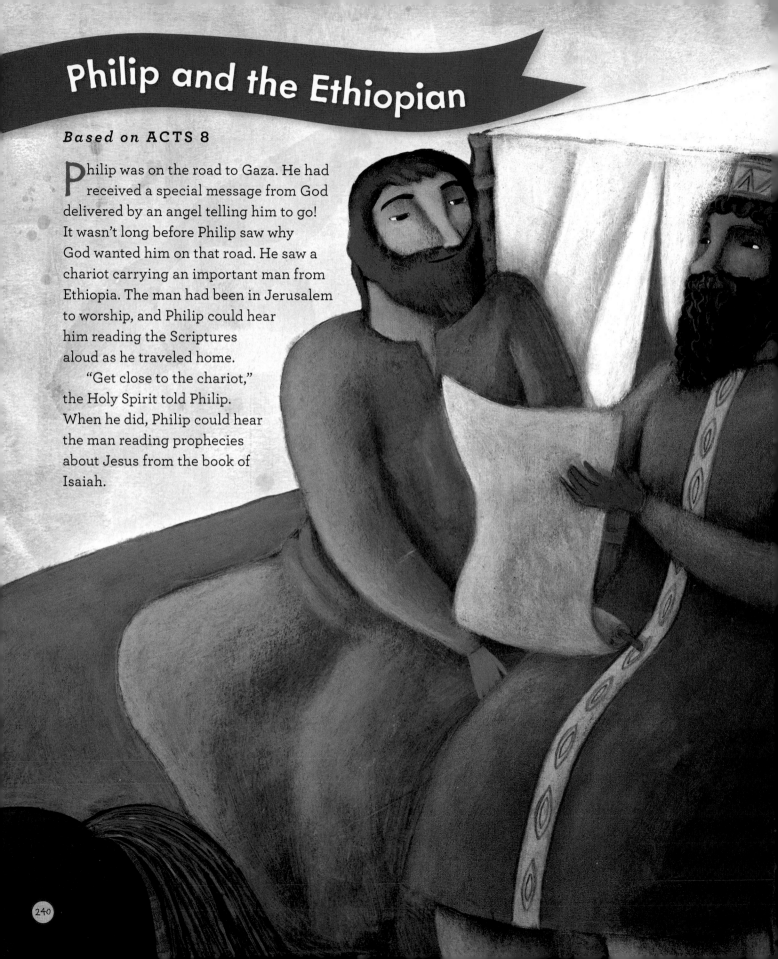

Philip and the Ethiopian

Based on **ACTS 8**

Philip was on the road to Gaza. He had received a special message from God delivered by an angel telling him to go! It wasn't long before Philip saw why God wanted him on that road. He saw a chariot carrying an important man from Ethiopia. The man had been in Jerusalem to worship, and Philip could hear him reading the Scriptures aloud as he traveled home.

"Get close to the chariot," the Holy Spirit told Philip. When he did, Philip could hear the man reading prophecies about Jesus from the book of Isaiah.

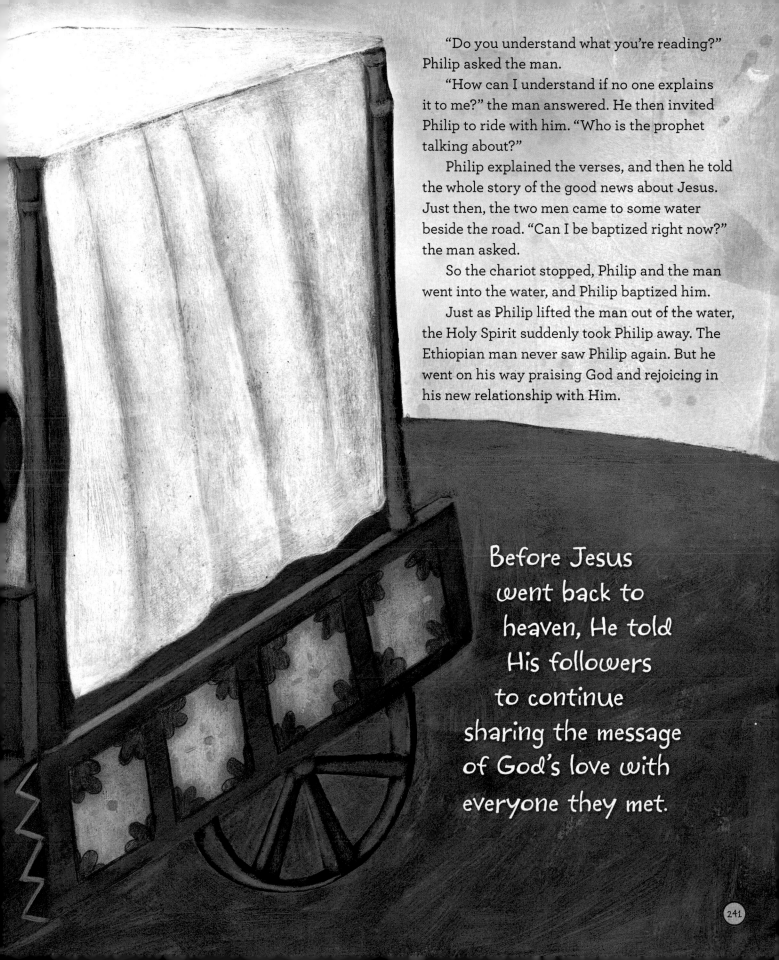

"Do you understand what you're reading?" Philip asked the man.

"How can I understand if no one explains it to me?" the man answered. He then invited Philip to ride with him. "Who is the prophet talking about?"

Philip explained the verses, and then he told the whole story of the good news about Jesus. Just then, the two men came to some water beside the road. "Can I be baptized right now?" the man asked.

So the chariot stopped, Philip and the man went into the water, and Philip baptized him.

Just as Philip lifted the man out of the water, the Holy Spirit suddenly took Philip away. The Ethiopian man never saw Philip again. But he went on his way praising God and rejoicing in his new relationship with Him.

Before Jesus went back to heaven, He told His followers to continue sharing the message of God's love with everyone they met.

Can't Stop Talking About Jesus

Nine-year-old Francisco Jr. can hardly wait for his father to return home from his fields so he can give him a big hug. In fact, when people see Francisco Sr., his son is often right beside him. Francisco Jr. likes learning about farming by watching his father grow corn, radishes, and beans. He also likes learning about Jesus by listening to his father tell other people about Him. Everywhere Francisco Sr. goes, he shares the good news that Jesus loves everyone!

Francisco Sr. didn't always talk about Jesus. When he first went to church in the little village of El Tablon, Honduras, it was just to make his wife, Carmen, happy. But in 2003, he began taking classes at church to learn how to be a better farmer. After class, the priest there explained to Francisco that believing in Jesus and following Him would help Francisco become a better husband and father. Francisco knew that he had not always been a very good person, but he wanted to be better. So Francisco asked Jesus to come into his life, to forgive all the bad things he had done, and to help him be the man Jesus wants him to be.

Now Francisco Sr. can't stop talking about Jesus and all the changes that have taken place in his life. Francisco is now the leader of three *ecclesiolas*, groups of people who meet to encourage one another to grow in their faith, and he and Carmen help 65 families in their community better understand how to live in a way that pleases Jesus. The families see what a big difference Jesus has made in Francisco's life, and they want to know Jesus too!

Father and son enjoy going to church and talking about Jesus.

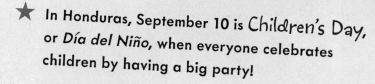

★ In Honduras, September 10 is Children's Day, or *Día del Niño*, when everyone celebrates children by having a big party!

★ The five stars on the Honduran flag represent the five countries in Central America.

Did you KNOW?

Children in Honduras celebrating at a birthday party.

243

Saul's Heart Is Changed

Based on ACTS 9

Grace and peace to you, brothers and sisters in Christ!" Paul loved Jesus so much that he spent all his time and energy teaching other people about Jesus and how to live in a way that pleases Him. In fact, God used Paul to write many of the books in the New Testament.

But Paul didn't always love and follow Jesus. Paul used to be called Saul, and when that was his name, he was one BIG bully! Saul didn't like Christians at all. In fact, every chance he got, Saul threw Christians in jail.

Saul was famous for hating Christians—and Christians were afraid of Saul. One day, Saul decided it wasn't enough to throw the believers in Jerusalem in jail. He thought, *I'll run* all *of the people who believe in Jesus out of our whole land!*

So Saul and his cruel friends set off for Damascus to round up all the Christians there. They hadn't gone far when a bright light shined down right on Saul and a loud voice boomed, "Saul, Saul, why are you trying to hurt Me?"

Saul fell to the ground. "Who is speaking to me?"

"I am Jesus, the One you are mistreating," the voice said.

Saul thought about this. *Can this be true? Is it possible that the Christians have been right all along and I'm the one who has been wrong? Yes, I am wrong. Jesus is God's Son.*

From that moment on, Saul's heart was changed. He trusted Jesus. Saul became the apostle Paul, and he traveled far and wide to tell everyone he could about Jesus.

God can change any heart.
Even the meanest bully can be changed by God's love.

A Change of Heart

Emmanuel lives with his mom, dad, and little brother, Abraham, in the African country of Ethiopia. Emmanuel doesn't remember a time when his father, Regassa, didn't love Jesus, but he's heard stories about how, when he was a young man, Regassa hated Jesus. And when Regassa hated Jesus, Regassa also hated all the people who loved Jesus.

But then Regassa got sick. For six years, he was unable to care for himself or his farm. Life got harder when his first wife died. He didn't even have the money he needed to prepare for her funeral.

But God's people knew about Regassa's suffering and helped him. They took Regassa to a church meeting, where he heard more about Jesus, and his heart began to soften. He found new friends, his illness went away, he started a new family, and he committed his life to following Jesus. Today Emmanuel's father is a happy man. Regassa's farm is so successful that he was named "Best Model Farmer" in his community.

God used a blinding light and a voice from heaven to change Saul's heart and convince him that Jesus is God's Son. God used hard times and some new Christian friends to do the same for Regassa.

★ In the ancient city of Lalibela, giant churches are carved out of stone deep under the ground.

★ *Injera* is a spongy, sour bread that is popular in Ethiopia. Since utensils are not used to pick up food, hungry children use a piece of *injera* instead of a fork!

Did you KNOW?

Once a man who hated Christians, Regassa has been completely changed.

Tabitha the Helper

Based on ACTS 9

Nooooo!" the women wailed. Their sweet friend Tabitha had died. Tabitha was one of the kindest people in town. She was always doing good and helping people who were poor. She made robes and other kinds of clothing to give to people who needed them. They appreciated her kindness and generosity. She took care of a lot of people.

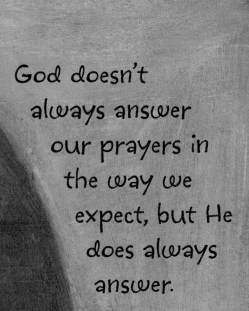

God doesn't always answer our prayers in the way we expect, but He does always answer.

When Tabitha got sick, her friends took care of her. When she died, they were heartbroken.

Then someone said, "I heard that Peter is in the next town. I know that God has helped him heal people before. Maybe he can bring Tabitha back to us. Why don't we ask him to come?"

When Peter arrived, Tabitha's friends and the people she had helped gathered around. They showed him the clothing she had made for them. They told him how kind and generous she was. They told him how much they would miss her.

Peter sent everyone out of the room. He knelt down beside Tabitha and prayed. Then he said, "Tabitha, get up!" Right away she opened her eyes and sat up! When Peter led her out to her friends, they cried tears of joy.

The story of Tabitha coming back to life spread quickly through the town, and many people believed in God because of it.

Hannah's Answered Prayer

Hannah was determined to find help for 100 children who live in places around the world where there might not be enough food to eat, clean water to drink, or a school to go to. She began by convincing her parents to support a little boy in Sri Lanka named Sandun. Then she set out to find sponsors for the other 99!

Sadly, before she could reach her goal, Hannah died in an accident. Everyone was heartbroken. Hannah had been very kind, and people loved her very much. Her parents received over 1,000 cards from friends telling them what a wonderful person Hannah was and how much they would miss her.

Hannah's parents had an idea. They wondered what would happen if all the people who had loved Hannah so much would help them reach Hannah's goal of finding 100 people to help 100 children. Inspired by Hannah's memory, many families signed up, and today their support provides money, prayers, and love for children in need around the world. Hannah's friend Brooke now sponsors Sandun in Sri Lanka. They exchange letters and tell each other about their lives and their families. They also write about how much they miss their friend Hannah.

Hannah prayed that God would send help for 100 children, and God answered her prayer.

Sandun misses Hannah, the girl who cared for him from many miles away.

★ Sri Lanka is known as the "Nation of Smiling People."

★ Hoppers are a popular snack in Sri Lanka made of pancakes served with eggs or honey and yogurt.

★ There is an elephant orphanage in Sri Lanka.

Did you KNOW?

Based on **ACTS 16**

These men are God's servants!" the slave girl ran through the streets shouting about Paul and Silas. "They are talking about how to be saved!" She shouted these things over and over, day after day. It wasn't really the girl who was doing this but an evil spirit that lived in her.

"Stop saying these things!" Paul told the spirit, but it wouldn't stop.

Finally Paul said, "In the name of Jesus Christ, I command you to come out of her!" The spirit left the girl, and she was quiet.

But the men who owned the girl were not happy because they made a lot of money by having her tell people's fortunes. They dragged Paul and Silas to the authorities and had them thrown into jail. Paul and Silas were beaten and chained to the cell in the middle of the jail.

So what did Paul and Silas do? They sang hymns and praised God. The other prisoners were amazed that Paul and Silas could praise God while chained in jail. But Paul and Silas weren't worried because they knew that their God was stronger than any jail cell.

Just then, a powerful earthquake

shook so hard that the prison doors fell off. The cell doors flew open. Chains fell off the prisoners' arms and legs. They all could have escaped, but they didn't. Paul encouraged everyone to stay.

Oh no! My boss will kill me if the prisoners have escaped! the jailer thought.

"We're all here!" Paul cried out. The jailer was amazed that the prisoners had stayed in the jail. He knew it was because of Paul and Silas. So he asked, "Sirs, how can I be saved?"

"You only need to believe on the Lord Jesus Christ," Paul said. The jailer believed and had Paul baptize him and his entire family!

God can open the doors—literally— for us to share Him with others. Be ready when they open!

An Open Door

The earth began to tremble, and buildings tumbled. By the time the shaking stopped, all that remained were piles of rocks and rubble on the side of the road. People had nowhere to live, nowhere to work, and nowhere to buy food for their families.

The people of Gujarat, India, hoped that someone would come to help them rebuild. Maybe neighboring villagers would arrive with some needed supplies. Perhaps important government officials would lend a hand. Instead, Christian friends started visiting, bringing food and construction materials to help the people of Gujarat start over. The people were very surprised. "We aren't Christians," they said, "but you are still willing to help us. Why?" The Christians were happy to tell them that they had come because they loved Jesus, because Jesus loved the people of Gujarat, and because Jesus wanted the people of Gujarat to know His love.

When an earthquake shook the jail where Paul and Silas were being held, the doors flew open and their chains fell off. Paul shared the good news about Jesus, and the jailer and his family were saved. When an earthquake shook Gujarat, God opened a different kind of door for Christian friends to tell the people there about God's love.

Christians help people in India after an earthquake.

Did you KNOW?

★ The national game of India is field hockey.

★ The Himalayas were named from the Sanskrit words *hima* ("snow") and *alaya* ("adobe"). They are home to the tallest mountains in the world and continue to grow each year!

The Armor of God

Based on 2 CORINTHIANS 11; EPHESIANS 6

Nothing could stop Paul from telling people about Jesus—not a shipwreck, not beatings, not even prison! And when Paul couldn't preach to the early Christians in person, he wrote them letters.

"Be strong in the Lord and in His power! Put on God's armor, so that when Satan attacks you, you can stand strong and continue to trust and obey God!" Paul told Jesus' followers.

Paul wanted the people to know that just as a soldier going into battle wears a suit of armor to protect himself, Jesus' followers also need protection. Then he listed six pieces of armor— belt, breastplate, shoes, shield, helmet, and sword—that

every Christian must put on to be safe in this world. But these are not ordinary pieces of armor. No, these pieces of armor stand for God's truth, righteousness, peace, faith, salvation, and Word.

Then, after God's people put on their armor, there is one more important thing they must do: pray! Paul knew that Satan will do everything he can to keep God's people from obeying and trusting God. The only way to win that battle is to put on the armor God gives us and pray for His help to keep us strong.

Start every day by putting on the full armor of God so that you will be ready to obey and trust Him. Remember that God is with you and He's fighting for you!

A Big Race

Based on **1 CORINTHIANS 9**

Paul once wrote that living the Christian life is like running a race. It's hard work. It requires lots of effort. And when the race is finished, there's a prize!

When runners prepare for a race, they go into strict training. They eat right, get plenty of rest, and exercise every day. Just like daily training is important for runners, it's also important for

Christians. When we try every day to worship and talk to God, to read God's Word and obey it, we grow closer to Him.

Then, on the day of the big race, all the runners line up together, keeping their eyes focused on the finish line. Each one wants to win the prize. At the end of the race, only one runner will receive a gold medal. But that's not true for Christians. When we keep our eyes on Jesus and live in a way that is pleasing to Him, we all get a prize! All of us who believe and trust God will have a crown in heaven—and that's a lot better than a gold medal. It is a crown that will last forever!

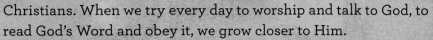

Live your life like a runner competing for a prize that will last forever. Worship and talk to God, read His Word, and try hard to obey it!

Running to Win

Do you like sports? Have you ever dreamed about competing in the Olympic Games? That was Nataly's dream, but her family was very poor, and she didn't think she would ever get a chance to represent El Salvador, the country where she lived, as an Olympic runner.

"Running in the hills and valleys was just an opportunity to take out the energy I had," explains Nataly. But it turns out that in addition to being energetic, Nataly was also very fast. When she was ten years old, she received help from World Vision friends so she could stay in school instead of having to go to work selling food from a cart. When people at her school saw how fast Nataly could run, they chose her to go to the National Sports Institute of El Salvador for special training. Nataly was a very hard worker, and in 2012, she ran for her country in the Olympic Games. She didn't win a medal, but she broke El Salvador's national record in her event!

When her World Vision friends began helping Nataly, they didn't know they were helping someone who would someday be an Olympic athlete. But they did know that helping people in need is something Jesus wants us to do. Nataly continues to pursue her dream of winning an Olympic medal.

God gave Nataly the ability to run fast.

Did you KNOW?

★ El Salvador is the smallest country in Central America.

★ San Salvador, the capital city, was nicknamed "the Valley of the Hammocks" because there are so many earthquakes that people needed beds to sway with the earth's movements.

Our Brother, Our Friend

Based on THE BOOK OF PHILEMON

Paul was a prisoner in Rome when he met an escaped slave named Onesimus. Onesimus had belonged to a man named Philemon, who was one of Paul's friends. Paul had taught Philemon about Jesus—and Paul had taught Onesimus too.

After Onesimus became a follower of Jesus, Onesimus was a very good helper to Paul, and Paul treated Onesimus like a son. Paul loved him very much, but he knew the right thing to do was to send him back to Philemon.

"Philemon," Paul wrote, "I know that Onesimus was your slave and that he escaped from you. But now he is your brother in the faith. Please welcome him like you would welcome me. If he owes you anything, charge it to me. I'll pay his debts. And I know, Philemon, that you'll do even more than I ask."

Paul asked Philemon to welcome Onesimus back as a brother, not a slave, and to treat Onesimus with kindness. After all, Onesimus was now a partner in the work of the Lord Jesus, just like Philemon and Paul.

We should treat all people, no matter who they are, what they look like, or what they have done in the past, with kindness and consideration.

263

God Loves Us Just As We Are

It hurt Neti's feelings when the people of Bathore, Albania, called him names. It wasn't his fault that he looked different from other children. When he was just a baby, Neti's face had been burned in an accident, and people still treated him badly because of his appearance. It made Neti very sad.

Then one day Neti heard about the International Day for Children with Disabilities. The Christian friends who had planned this special day hoped that it would be a time when children with disabilities could make new friends. Neti was excited to be a part of this event, and for the first time in his life, he felt "comfortable and important."

Besmira, one of the helpers, said that when she met Neti, she knew he was "intelligent and lively." She also said that all the children at the celebration wanted to spend time with him. Neti only wished that all children were as nice as those he met on that special day.

Besmira hopes that being with other children who treat him with kindness and respect will help Neti understand that the way he looks is not important. She wants him to know that God loves him just the way he is.

God is not concerned with who we are or what we look like or even, as in the case of Onesimus, what we have done in the past. By surrounding himself with Christian friends and with other children with disabilities, Neti is beginning to learn that we are all precious in God's sight.

Neti

Children learning that they are precious in God's sight.

Did you KNOW?

★ Traditional Albanian men's clothing includes a white kilt, called a *fustanella*, and a white felt hat, called a *qeleshe*. The hats have different shapes depending upon where in Albania they come from.

★ Albanians love to eat *byrek me spinak*, a traditional spinach and cheese pie.

★ A two-headed black eagle sits in the center of the Albanian flag. He is said to faithfully watch over and guide the king.

The King Returns!

Based on THE BOOK OF REVELATION

D o you know about Jesus? Let me tell you about my Friend."
The apostle John loved Jesus so much that he kept telling *everyone* about Jesus. Over and over, the religious leaders, who didn't like Jesus at all, told John to stop talking. When he didn't, they sent John to live alone on the faraway island of Patmos.

While he was on Patmos, John had an amazing dream. It was a dream God gave him about the future.

Heaven is a wonderful place where there is never pain or sadness. And the best thing about heaven is that God, who loves us more than we can ever imagine, is there and we will be with Him.

In John's dream, he saw great battles and terrible storms. Satan was doing everything he could to get people to turn away from God. But the dream promised that Jesus would come again for everyone who has believed in Him and faithfully followed Him. In fact, followers of Jesus don't need to be afraid of the future because we know who will win the battle—our great God!

The last part of John's dream was the best part. He saw heaven, where there will be a great crowd of people from every nation on earth shouting happy praises to God. God will wipe away every tear, and there will be no more sadness or pain or death.

The good news is that Jesus is coming back, and then those who have trusted and obeyed God will live in heaven with Him forever!

Doing God's Work While We Wait

Jesus promised that someday He will return, but until He does, we have a job to do. Our job is to love God and to love our neighbors.

We show our love for God by worshipping and praising Him. We also show our love for God by loving and caring for the people He created. Sometimes loving others—even people we don't know—means making sure they have food, clean water, and a safe place to live. Sometimes loving other people means taking time to be kind.

This is the work Jesus left for us to do. It's not an easy job. But when we show our love for God by helping others, people will know how much Jesus loves them.

God wants to use us to show the people of the world just how much He loves them. It is a big job, but He will guide you every step of the way!

ZAMBIA

How Can We Help?

Sometimes the problems in our world seem very big. So many children don't have food or water or a place to live. There is no school in their town and no doctor to go to when they get sick. But lots of other children around the world have all those things. How can the children who have so much help the children who have so little?

The students at Wheaton Academy in West Chicago, Illinois, wanted to answer that important question, so they began to pray. They asked God to show them what He wanted them to do. They thought they had the answer when they found a World Vision catalog full of things that children around the world needed. On one page was a photograph of a school. The little village of Kakolo, Zambia, needed a school, but the catalog said it would cost $53,000. That was a lot of money, and these students didn't have anywhere near enough. Even so, they were sure that God was asking them to buy a school for the kids in Zambia.

They started raising money. They had a dodgeball tournament. They hosted a talent show. They took the money they would have spent on themselves and put it into a special fund. To everyone's surprise, by the end of the year, they had raised more than enough money to pay for the school!

But the bigger surprise was how much the students at Wheaton Academy had grown to love the children of Kakolo. By praying for them and working hard to help them, the American students had fallen in love with a village halfway around the world. God put it in their hearts to serve others, and when they obeyed, they were blessed. Not everyone can build a school, but we can all do something to make our world a better place. Ask God to show you what you can do!

Wheaton Academy students found out how much they could do to make a difference for kids in Zambia.

270

Did you KNOW?

★ Kakolo is located near the Zambia–Tanzania border.

★ Most of the people of Zambia are Bantu and speak Bemba. Zambians also speak over 70 other languages.

★ Zambians usually live with their extended families in houses grouped together so they can help one another.

A Prayer for Children Everywhere

Our dear Father in heaven,
We thank You for who You are and all that You have done for us.
　We pray that we will know You
　　　And that, as we grow, we will become more like You.
　　　Please use us to do your work in the world:
　　　To cover each child who is cold with a warm blanket and a safe house,
　To give each child who is sick the medicine needed,
To fill each child who is hungry and thirsty with fresh food and clean water,
　To bring books and education to those who have no place to learn.
　Please be with every child who is cold,
　And warm them with Your love.
　Please be with every child who is sick,
　And touch them with Your healing hand.
　Please be with every child who is hungry,
　And fill them with the Bread of Life.
　Please be with every child who is thirsty,
　And quench their thirst with Living Water.
　Please be with every child who needs to know the Savior,
　　　And teach them from Your Holy Word about the God who loves them so.
　　　In Jesus' name,
　　　Amen.